THIS JOURNAL
BELONGS TO:

_____

UNPLUG

IN TODAY'S HYPERCONNECTED WORLD, IT IS EASY FOR EVEN THE MOST MINDFUL OF US TO BECOME OVER-RELIANT ON TECHNOLOGY. FROM CELL PHONES TO COMPUTERS TO TELEVISION, SOME STUDIES ESTIMATE THAT AMERICANS SPEND UP TO ELEVEN HOURS A DAY INTERACTING WITH SCREEN-BASED MEDIA. SOMETIMES FRAMED AS TECHNOLOGY "ADDICTION," THIS OVERDEPENDENCE HAS BEEN LINKED TO A HOST OF MENTAL HEALTH ISSUES, INCLUDING DEPRESSION, ANXIETY, AND LONELINESS. THE GOOD NEWS IS THAT MORE AND MORE PEOPLE ARE RECOGNIZING THE NEGATIVE SIDE EFFECTS OF THEIR TECH USE, AND THEY ARE TRYING TO CORRECT IT. MORE AND MORE PEOPLE ARE LOOKING TO UNPLUG.

THAT'S WHERE THIS JOURNAL COMES IN. FOR MOST ADULTS, USING TECHNOLOGY IS AN UNAVOIDABLE PART OF THEIR DAILY WORK LIFE. IT IS IN OUR NONWORKING HOURS, OUR HOME TIME, AND OUR PERSONAL LIVES WHERE WE CAN MAKE MORE EFFORTS TO GET "OFF-SCREEN." WHILE THERE ARE PLENTY OF APPS AND SYSTEMS FOR TRACKING YOUR ON-SCREEN TIME, THIS JOURNAL WILL HELP YOU PLAN, TRACK, AND RECORD YOUR OFF-SCREEN TIME, ENCOURAGING YOU TO SPEND A LITTLE TIME EACH DAY IN NON-SCREEN-BASED ACTIVITIES. EACH MORNING, YOU WILL WRITE DOWN YOUR GOAL OFF-SCREEN TIME AND FILL IN YOUR "DAILY OFF-SCREEN PLANNER," SETTING ASIDE WHATEVER TIME YOU CAN FOR SPECIFIC OFF-SCREEN PURSUITS. THE PLANNER IS DIVIDED INTO TEN CATEGORIES, WHICH FUNCTION AS SUGGESTIONS FOR HOW YOU CAN SPEND YOUR TIME:

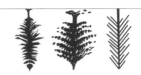

- **EXPLORE:** Go somewhere new. Take a hike, visit a new part of town, or try a new restaurant.
- **MEET:** Connect with someone face-to-face. Spend time with friends or loved ones in the real world instead of the virtual one.
- **MOVE:** Do something active. Visit the gym, go dancing, or just take a fifteen-minute walk—without your phone.
- **CREATE:** Make something with your hands. Draw, cook, or play an instrument—do something artistic.
- **LEARN:** Read a book, visit a museum, or attend a lecture. Or just do a crossword. Stretch your mind.
- **REFLECT:** Do something introspective. Visit a spiritual institution. Journal, meditate, or pray.
- **HELP:** Do something for another person. Support a good cause. Donate time to a nonprofit or charity.
- **PLAY:** Host a board game night, climb a tree, or take your pet to the park.
- **PREP:** Run errands, do chores, or make a grocery list—make time to care for the infrastructure of your daily life.
- **OTHER:** Anything and everything else that doesn't include a screen.

This journal also provides space at the end of the day to reflect on your successes and challenges and to assess the impact your off-screen time had on your mood. While it's not necessary (or realistic!) to do something in every one of these categories every day, doing something in at least one of them can have an extremely positive effect on your mental health. You may find it gets easier and easier to put down your phone, head outside, and reconnect with yourself and the real world.

MORNING

GOAL: TODAY, I WILL SPEND __6__ HOUR(S) OFF-SCREE

DAILY OFF-SCREEN PLANNER

EXPLORE	MEET
	go to outlets w/ Syd, delaney, Abby
TIME:	TIME: 3:00pm
MOVE	CREATE
run and workout	new notebooks
TIME:	TIME:
LEARN	REFLECT
TIME:	TIME:
HELP	PLAY
TIME:	TIME:
PREP	OTHER
TIME:	TIME:

EVENING

TODAY I SPENT _____ HOUR(S) OFF-SCREEN.

WHAT I ENJOYED MOST FROM MY OFF-SCREEN TIME:

_____

_____

_____

_____

CHALLENGES: _____

_____

_____

_____

MY OVERALL MOOD TODAY:

☐ CHEERFUL   ☐ ANXIOUS   ☐ HOPEFUL

☐ CALM   ☐ TIRED   ☐ TENSE

☐ LIGHTHEARTED   ☐ MOTIVATED   ☐ BORED

☐ GLOOMY   ☐ LAZY   ☐ CONFIDENT

☐ STRESSED   ☐ REFLECTIVE   ☐ GRATEFUL

☐ ANGRY   ☐ ROMANTIC   ☐ OTHER: _____

FINAL THOUGHTS: _____

_____

_____

_____

_____

MORNING

GOAL: TODAY, I WILL SPEND _____ HOUR(S) OFF-SCREE

DAILY OFF-SCREEN PLANNER

EXPLORE	MEET
TIME:	TIME:
MOVE	CREATE
TIME:	TIME:
LEARN	REFLECT
TIME:	TIME:
HELP	PLAY
TIME:	TIME:
PREP	OTHER
TIME:	TIME:

EVENING

TODAY I SPENT _____ HOUR(S) OFF-SCREEN.

WHAT I ENJOYED MOST FROM MY OFF-SCREEN TIME:

_____

_____

_____

_____

_____

CHALLENGES:

_____

_____

_____

_____

MY OVERALL MOOD TODAY:

☐ CHEERFUL   ☐ ANXIOUS   ☐ HOPEFUL
☐ CALM   ☐ TIRED   ☐ TENSE
☐ LIGHTHEARTED   ☐ MOTIVATED   ☐ BORED
☐ GLOOMY   ☐ LAZY   ☐ CONFIDENT
☐ STRESSED   ☐ REFLECTIVE   ☐ GRATEFUL
☐ ANGRY   ☐ ROMANTIC   ☐ OTHER: _____

FINAL THOUGHTS:

_____

_____

_____

_____

_____

MORNING

GOAL: TODAY, I WILL SPEND _____ HOUR(S) OFF-SCREEN

DAILY OFF-SCREEN PLANNER

EXPLORE	MEET
TIME:	TIME:
MOVE	CREATE
TIME:	TIME:
LEARN	REFLECT
TIME:	TIME:
HELP	PLAY
TIME:	TIME:
PREP	OTHER
TIME:	TIME:

EVENING

TODAY I SPENT _____ HOUR(S) OFF-SCREEN.

WHAT I ENJOYED MOST FROM MY OFF-SCREEN TIME:
_____
_____
_____
_____
_____

CHALLENGES:
_____
_____
_____
_____

MY OVERALL MOOD TODAY:

☐ CHEERFUL   ☐ ANXIOUS   ☐ HOPEFUL
☐ CALM   ☐ TIRED   ☐ TENSE
☐ LIGHTHEARTED   ☐ MOTIVATED   ☐ BORED
☐ GLOOMY   ☐ LAZY   ☐ CONFIDENT
☐ STRESSED   ☐ REFLECTIVE   ☐ GRATEFUL
☐ ANGRY   ☐ ROMANTIC   ☐ OTHER: _____

FINAL THOUGHTS:
_____
_____
_____
_____

MORNING

DATE __/__/__

GOAL: TODAY, I WILL SPEND _____ HOUR(S) OFF-SCREEN

DAILY OFF-SCREEN PLANNER

EXPLORE TIME:	MEET TIME:
MOVE TIME:	CREATE TIME:
LEARN TIME:	REFLECT TIME:
HELP TIME:	PLAY TIME:
PREP TIME:	OTHER TIME:

EVENING

TODAY I SPENT _____ HOUR(S) OFF-SCREEN.

WHAT I ENJOYED MOST FROM MY OFF-SCREEN TIME:
_____
_____
_____
_____
_____

CHALLENGES:
_____
_____
_____
_____
_____

MY OVERALL MOOD TODAY:

- ☐ CHEERFUL
- ☐ CALM
- ☐ LIGHTHEARTED
- ☐ GLOOMY
- ☐ STRESSED
- ☐ ANGRY

- ☐ ANXIOUS
- ☐ TIRED
- ☐ MOTIVATED
- ☐ LAZY
- ☐ REFLECTIVE
- ☐ ROMANTIC

- ☐ HOPEFUL
- ☐ TENSE
- ☐ BORED
- ☐ CONFIDENT
- ☐ GRATEFUL
- ☐ OTHER: _____

FINAL THOUGHTS:
_____
_____
_____
_____
_____

MORNING

DATE _/_/_

GOAL: TODAY, I WILL SPEND _____ HOUR(S) OFF-SCREEN

DAILY OFF-SCREEN PLANNER

EXPLORE	MEET
TIME:	TIME:
MOVE	CREATE
TIME:	TIME:
LEARN	REFLECT
TIME:	TIME:
HELP	PLAY
TIME:	TIME:
PREP	OTHER
TIME:	TIME:

EVENING

TODAY I SPENT _____ HOUR(S) OFF-SCREEN.

WHAT I ENJOYED MOST FROM MY OFF-SCREEN TIME:
_____
_____
_____
_____
_____

CHALLENGES: _____
_____
_____
_____

MY OVERALL MOOD TODAY:

- [ ] CHEERFUL
- [ ] CALM
- [ ] LIGHTHEARTED
- [ ] GLOOMY
- [ ] STRESSED
- [ ] ANGRY

- [ ] ANXIOUS
- [ ] TIRED
- [ ] MOTIVATED
- [ ] LAZY
- [ ] REFLECTIVE
- [ ] ROMANTIC

- [ ] HOPEFUL
- [ ] TENSE
- [ ] BORED
- [ ] CONFIDENT
- [ ] GRATEFUL
- [ ] OTHER: _____

FINAL THOUGHTS: _____
_____
_____
_____
_____

MORNING

GOAL: TODAY, I WILL SPEND _____ HOUR(S) OFF-SCREEN

DAILY OFF-SCREEN PLANNER

EXPLORE	MEET
TIME:	TIME:
MOVE	CREATE
TIME:	TIME:
LEARN	REFLECT
TIME:	TIME:
HELP	PLAY
TIME:	TIME:
PREP	OTHER
TIME:	TIME:

EVENING

TODAY I SPENT _____ HOUR(S) OFF-SCREEN.

WHAT I ENJOYED MOST FROM MY OFF-SCREEN TIME:
_____
_____
_____
_____
_____

CHALLENGES:
_____
_____
_____
_____

MY OVERALL MOOD TODAY:

☐ CHEERFUL   ☐ ANXIOUS   ☐ HOPEFUL
☐ CALM   ☐ TIRED   ☐ TENSE
☐ LIGHTHEARTED   ☐ MOTIVATED   ☐ BORED
☐ GLOOMY   ☐ LAZY   ☐ CONFIDENT
☐ STRESSED   ☐ REFLECTIVE   ☐ GRATEFUL
☐ ANGRY   ☐ ROMANTIC   ☐ OTHER: _____

FINAL THOUGHTS:
_____
_____
_____
_____

MORNING

GOAL: TODAY, I WILL SPEND _____ HOUR(S) OFF-SCREEN

DAILY OFF-SCREEN PLANNER

EXPLORE TIME:	MEET TIME:
MOVE TIME:	CREATE TIME:
LEARN TIME:	REFLECT TIME:
HELP TIME:	PLAY TIME:
PREP TIME:	OTHER TIME:

EVENING

TODAY I SPENT _____ HOUR(S) OFF-SCREEN.

WHAT I ENJOYED MOST FROM MY OFF-SCREEN TIME:
_____
_____
_____
_____
_____

CHALLENGES:
_____
_____
_____
_____

MY OVERALL MOOD TODAY:

☐ CHEERFUL   ☐ ANXIOUS   ☐ HOPEFUL
☐ CALM   ☐ TIRED   ☐ TENSE
☐ LIGHTHEARTED   ☐ MOTIVATED   ☐ BORED
☐ GLOOMY   ☐ LAZY   ☐ CONFIDENT
☐ STRESSED   ☐ REFLECTIVE   ☐ GRATEFUL
☐ ANGRY   ☐ ROMANTIC   ☐ OTHER: _____

FINAL THOUGHTS:
_____
_____
_____
_____

MORNING

GOAL: TODAY, I WILL SPEND _____ HOUR(S) OFF-SCREEN

DAILY OFF-SCREEN PLANNER

EXPLORE	MEET
TIME:	TIME:
MOVE	CREATE
TIME:	TIME:
LEARN	REFLECT
TIME:	TIME:
HELP	PLAY
TIME:	TIME:
PREP	OTHER
TIME:	TIME:

EVENING

TODAY I SPENT _____ HOUR(S) OFF-SCREEN.

WHAT I ENJOYED MOST FROM MY OFF-SCREEN TIME:

_____

_____

_____

_____

_____

CHALLENGES:

_____

_____

_____

_____

MY OVERALL MOOD TODAY:

☐ CHEERFUL   ☐ ANXIOUS   ☐ HOPEFUL
☐ CALM   ☐ TIRED   ☐ TENSE
☐ LIGHTHEARTED   ☐ MOTIVATED   ☐ BORED
☐ GLOOMY   ☐ LAZY   ☐ CONFIDENT
☐ STRESSED   ☐ REFLECTIVE   ☐ GRATEFUL
☐ ANGRY   ☐ ROMANTIC   ☐ OTHER: _____

FINAL THOUGHTS:

_____

_____

_____

_____

MORNING

GOAL: TODAY, I WILL SPEND _____ HOUR(S) OFF-SCREEN

DAILY OFF-SCREEN PLANNER

EXPLORE	MEET
TIME:	TIME:
MOVE	CREATE
TIME:	TIME:
LEARN	REFLECT
TIME:	TIME:
HELP	PLAY
TIME:	TIME:
PREP	OTHER
TIME:	TIME:

EVENING

TODAY I SPENT _____ HOUR(S) OFF-SCREEN.

WHAT I ENJOYED MOST FROM MY OFF-SCREEN TIME:
_____
_____
_____
_____
_____

CHALLENGES:
_____
_____
_____
_____

MY OVERALL MOOD TODAY:

☐ CHEERFUL   ☐ ANXIOUS   ☐ HOPEFUL
☐ CALM   ☐ TIRED   ☐ TENSE
☐ LIGHTHEARTED   ☐ MOTIVATED   ☐ BORED
☐ GLOOMY   ☐ LAZY   ☐ CONFIDENT
☐ STRESSED   ☐ REFLECTIVE   ☐ GRATEFUL
☐ ANGRY   ☐ ROMANTIC   ☐ OTHER: _____

FINAL THOUGHTS:
_____
_____
_____
_____

MORNING

GOAL: TODAY, I WILL SPEND _____ HOUR(S) OFF-SCREEN

DAILY OFF-SCREEN PLANNER

EXPLORE	MEET
TIME:	TIME:
MOVE	CREATE
TIME:	TIME:
LEARN	REFLECT
TIME:	TIME:
HELP	PLAY
TIME:	TIME:
PREP	OTHER
TIME:	TIME:

EVENING

TODAY I SPENT _____ HOUR(S) OFF-SCREEN.

WHAT I ENJOYED MOST FROM MY OFF-SCREEN TIME:

_____

_____

_____

_____

CHALLENGES:

_____

_____

_____

MY OVERALL MOOD TODAY:

- [ ] CHEERFUL
- [ ] CALM
- [ ] LIGHTHEARTED
- [ ] GLOOMY
- [ ] STRESSED
- [ ] ANGRY

- [ ] ANXIOUS
- [ ] TIRED
- [ ] MOTIVATED
- [ ] LAZY
- [ ] REFLECTIVE
- [ ] ROMANTIC

- [ ] HOPEFUL
- [ ] TENSE
- [ ] BORED
- [ ] CONFIDENT
- [ ] GRATEFUL
- [ ] OTHER: _____

FINAL THOUGHTS:

_____

_____

_____

_____

MORNING

GOAL: TODAY, I WILL SPEND _____ HOUR(S) OFF-SCREEN

DAILY OFF-SCREEN PLANNER

EXPLORE	MEET
TIME:	TIME:
MOVE	CREATE
TIME:	TIME:
LEARN	REFLECT
TIME:	TIME:
HELP	PLAY
TIME:	TIME:
PREP	OTHER
TIME:	TIME:

EVENING

TODAY I SPENT _____ HOUR(S) OFF-SCREEN.

WHAT I ENJOYED MOST FROM MY OFF-SCREEN TIME:

_____

_____

_____

_____

CHALLENGES:

_____

_____

_____

_____

MY OVERALL MOOD TODAY:

☐ CHEERFUL   ☐ ANXIOUS   ☐ HOPEFUL

☐ CALM   ☐ TIRED   ☐ TENSE

☐ LIGHTHEARTED   ☐ MOTIVATED   ☐ BORED

☐ GLOOMY   ☐ LAZY   ☐ CONFIDENT

☐ STRESSED   ☐ REFLECTIVE   ☐ GRATEFUL

☐ ANGRY   ☐ ROMANTIC   ☐ OTHER: _____

FINAL THOUGHTS:

_____

_____

_____

_____

MORNING

GOAL: TODAY, I WILL SPEND _____ HOUR(S) OFF-SCREEN

DAILY OFF-SCREEN PLANNER

EXPLORE	MEET
TIME:	TIME:
MOVE	CREATE
TIME:	TIME:
LEARN	REFLECT
TIME:	TIME:
HELP	PLAY
TIME:	TIME:
PREP	OTHER
TIME:	TIME:

EVENING

TODAY I SPENT _____ HOUR(S) OFF-SCREEN.

WHAT I ENJOYED MOST FROM MY OFF-SCREEN TIME:

_____
_____
_____
_____
_____

CHALLENGES:

_____
_____
_____
_____

MY OVERALL MOOD TODAY:

- ☐ CHEERFUL
- ☐ CALM
- ☐ LIGHTHEARTED
- ☐ GLOOMY
- ☐ STRESSED
- ☐ ANGRY

- ☐ ANXIOUS
- ☐ TIRED
- ☐ MOTIVATED
- ☐ LAZY
- ☐ REFLECTIVE
- ☐ ROMANTIC

- ☐ HOPEFUL
- ☐ TENSE
- ☐ BORED
- ☐ CONFIDENT
- ☐ GRATEFUL
- ☐ OTHER: _____

FINAL THOUGHTS:

_____
_____
_____
_____
_____

MORNING

GOAL: TODAY, I WILL SPEND _____ HOUR(S) OFF-SCREEN

DAILY OFF-SCREEN PLANNER

EXPLORE	MEET
TIME:	TIME:
MOVE	CREATE
TIME:	TIME:
LEARN	REFLECT
TIME:	TIME:
HELP	PLAY
TIME:	TIME:
PREP	OTHER
TIME:	TIME:

EVENING

TODAY I SPENT _____ HOUR(S) OFF-SCREEN.

WHAT I ENJOYED MOST FROM MY OFF-SCREEN TIME:

_____
_____
_____
_____
_____

CHALLENGES:

_____
_____
_____
_____

MY OVERALL MOOD TODAY:

- ☐ CHEERFUL
- ☐ CALM
- ☐ LIGHTHEARTED
- ☐ GLOOMY
- ☐ STRESSED
- ☐ ANGRY

- ☐ ANXIOUS
- ☐ TIRED
- ☐ MOTIVATED
- ☐ LAZY
- ☐ REFLECTIVE
- ☐ ROMANTIC

- ☐ HOPEFUL
- ☐ TENSE
- ☐ BORED
- ☐ CONFIDENT
- ☐ GRATEFUL
- ☐ OTHER: _____

FINAL THOUGHTS:

_____
_____
_____
_____
_____

MORNING

GOAL: TODAY, I WILL SPEND _____ HOUR(S) OFF-SCREEN

DAILY OFF-SCREEN PLANNER

EXPLORE	MEET
TIME:	TIME:
MOVE	CREATE
TIME:	TIME:
LEARN	REFLECT
TIME:	TIME:
HELP	PLAY
TIME:	TIME:
PREP	OTHER
TIME:	TIME:

EVENING

TODAY I SPENT _____ HOUR(S) OFF-SCREEN.

WHAT I ENJOYED MOST FROM MY OFF-SCREEN TIME:

_____

_____

_____

_____

CHALLENGES:

_____

_____

_____

MY OVERALL MOOD TODAY:

☐ CHEERFUL   ☐ ANXIOUS   ☐ HOPEFUL
☐ CALM   ☐ TIRED   ☐ TENSE
☐ LIGHTHEARTED   ☐ MOTIVATED   ☐ BORED
☐ GLOOMY   ☐ LAZY   ☐ CONFIDENT
☐ STRESSED   ☐ REFLECTIVE   ☐ GRATEFUL
☐ ANGRY   ☐ ROMANTIC   ☐ OTHER: _____

FINAL THOUGHTS:

_____

_____

_____

_____

MORNING

GOAL: TODAY, I WILL SPEND _____ HOUR(S) OFF-SCREE

DAILY OFF-SCREEN PLANNER

EXPLORE	MEET
TIME:	TIME:
MOVE	CREATE
TIME:	TIME:
LEARN	REFLECT
TIME:	TIME:
HELP	PLAY
TIME:	TIME:
PREP	OTHER
TIME:	TIME:

EVENING

TODAY I SPENT _____ HOUR(S) OFF-SCREEN.

WHAT I ENJOYED MOST FROM MY OFF-SCREEN TIME:

_____
_____
_____
_____

CHALLENGES:

_____
_____
_____
_____

MY OVERALL MOOD TODAY:

☐ CHEERFUL   ☐ ANXIOUS   ☐ HOPEFUL
☐ CALM   ☐ TIRED   ☐ TENSE
☐ LIGHTHEARTED   ☐ MOTIVATED   ☐ BORED
☐ GLOOMY   ☐ LAZY   ☐ CONFIDENT
☐ STRESSED   ☐ REFLECTIVE   ☐ GRATEFUL
☐ ANGRY   ☐ ROMANTIC   ☐ OTHER: _____

FINAL THOUGHTS:

_____
_____
_____
_____

MORNING

GOAL: TODAY, I WILL SPEND _____ HOUR(S) OFF-SCREEN

DAILY OFF-SCREEN PLANNER

EXPLORE	MEET
TIME:	TIME:
MOVE	CREATE
TIME:	TIME:
LEARN	REFLECT
TIME:	TIME:
HELP	PLAY
TIME:	TIME:
PREP	OTHER
TIME:	TIME:

EVENING

TODAY I SPENT _____ HOUR(S) OFF-SCREEN.

WHAT I ENJOYED MOST FROM MY OFF-SCREEN TIME:
_____
_____
_____
_____
_____

CHALLENGES: _____
_____
_____
_____
_____

MY OVERALL MOOD TODAY:

☐ CHEERFUL   ☐ ANXIOUS   ☐ HOPEFUL

☐ CALM   ☐ TIRED   ☐ TENSE

☐ LIGHTHEARTED   ☐ MOTIVATED   ☐ BORED

☐ GLOOMY   ☐ LAZY   ☐ CONFIDENT

☐ STRESSED   ☐ REFLECTIVE   ☐ GRATEFUL

☐ ANGRY   ☐ ROMANTIC   ☐ OTHER: _____

FINAL THOUGHTS: _____
_____
_____
_____

MORNING

GOAL: TODAY, I WILL SPEND _____ HOUR(S) OFF-SCREEN

DAILY OFF-SCREEN PLANNER

EXPLORE	MEET
TIME:	TIME:
MOVE	CREATE
TIME:	TIME:
LEARN	REFLECT
TIME:	TIME:
HELP	PLAY
TIME:	TIME:
PREP	OTHER
TIME:	TIME:

EVENING

TODAY I SPENT _____ HOUR(S) OFF-SCREEN.

WHAT I ENJOYED MOST FROM MY OFF-SCREEN TIME:

_____

_____

_____

CHALLENGES:

_____

_____

_____

MY OVERALL MOOD TODAY:

- ☐ CHEERFUL
- ☐ CALM
- ☐ LIGHTHEARTED
- ☐ GLOOMY
- ☐ STRESSED
- ☐ ANGRY

- ☐ ANXIOUS
- ☐ TIRED
- ☐ MOTIVATED
- ☐ LAZY
- ☐ REFLECTIVE
- ☐ ROMANTIC

- ☐ HOPEFUL
- ☐ TENSE
- ☐ BORED
- ☐ CONFIDENT
- ☐ GRATEFUL
- ☐ OTHER: _____

FINAL THOUGHTS:

_____

_____

_____

MORNING

GOAL: TODAY, I WILL SPEND _____ HOUR(S) OFF-SCREEN

DAILY OFF-SCREEN PLANNER

EXPLORE	MEET
TIME:	TIME:
MOVE	CREATE
TIME:	TIME:
LEARN	REFLECT
TIME:	TIME:
HELP	PLAY
TIME:	TIME:
PREP	OTHER
TIME:	TIME:

EVENING

TODAY I SPENT _____ HOUR(S) OFF-SCREEN.

WHAT I ENJOYED MOST FROM MY OFF-SCREEN TIME:

_____

_____

_____

_____

CHALLENGES:

_____

_____

_____

_____

MY OVERALL MOOD TODAY:

☐ CHEERFUL   ☐ ANXIOUS   ☐ HOPEFUL

☐ CALM   ☐ TIRED   ☐ TENSE

☐ LIGHTHEARTED   ☐ MOTIVATED   ☐ BORED

☐ GLOOMY   ☐ LAZY   ☐ CONFIDENT

☐ STRESSED   ☐ REFLECTIVE   ☐ GRATEFUL

☐ ANGRY   ☐ ROMANTIC   ☐ OTHER: _____

FINAL THOUGHTS:

_____

_____

_____

_____

MORNING

GOAL: TODAY, I WILL SPEND _____ HOUR(S) OFF-SCREEN

DAILY OFF-SCREEN PLANNER

EXPLORE	MEET
TIME:	TIME:
MOVE	CREATE
TIME:	TIME:
LEARN	REFLECT
TIME:	TIME:
HELP	PLAY
TIME:	TIME:
PREP	OTHER
TIME:	TIME:

EVENING

TODAY I SPENT _____ HOUR(S) OFF-SCREEN.

WHAT I ENJOYED MOST FROM MY OFF-SCREEN TIME:
_____
_____
_____
_____
_____

CHALLENGES:
_____
_____
_____
_____

MY OVERALL MOOD TODAY:

☐ CHEERFUL   ☐ ANXIOUS   ☐ HOPEFUL
☐ CALM   ☐ TIRED   ☐ TENSE
☐ LIGHTHEARTED   ☐ MOTIVATED   ☐ BORED
☐ GLOOMY   ☐ LAZY   ☐ CONFIDENT
☐ STRESSED   ☐ REFLECTIVE   ☐ GRATEFUL
☐ ANGRY   ☐ ROMANTIC   ☐ OTHER: _____

FINAL THOUGHTS:
_____
_____
_____
_____

MORNING

GOAL: TODAY, I WILL SPEND _____ HOUR(S) OFF-SCREEN

DAILY OFF-SCREEN PLANNER

EXPLORE	MEET
TIME:	TIME:
MOVE	CREATE
TIME:	TIME:
LEARN	REFLECT
TIME:	TIME:
HELP	PLAY
TIME:	TIME:
PREP	OTHER
TIME:	TIME:

EVENING

TODAY I SPENT _____ HOUR(S) OFF-SCREEN.

WHAT I ENJOYED MOST FROM MY OFF-SCREEN TIME:
_____
_____
_____
_____
_____

CHALLENGES:
_____
_____
_____
_____
_____

MY OVERALL MOOD TODAY:

☐ CHEERFUL   ☐ ANXIOUS   ☐ HOPEFUL
☐ CALM   ☐ TIRED   ☐ TENSE
☐ LIGHTHEARTED   ☐ MOTIVATED   ☐ BORED
☐ GLOOMY   ☐ LAZY   ☐ CONFIDENT
☐ STRESSED   ☐ REFLECTIVE   ☐ GRATEFUL
☐ ANGRY   ☐ ROMANTIC   ☐ OTHER: _____

FINAL THOUGHTS:
_____
_____
_____
_____
_____

MORNING

GOAL: TODAY, I WILL SPEND _____ HOUR(S) OFF-SCREEN

DAILY OFF-SCREEN PLANNER

EXPLORE	MEET
TIME:	TIME:
MOVE	CREATE
TIME:	TIME:
LEARN	REFLECT
TIME:	TIME:
HELP	PLAY
TIME:	TIME:
PREP	OTHER
TIME:	TIME:

EVENING

TODAY I SPENT _____ HOUR(S) OFF-SCREEN.

WHAT I ENJOYED MOST FROM MY OFF-SCREEN TIME:

_____
_____
_____
_____
_____

CHALLENGES:

_____
_____
_____
_____
_____

MY OVERALL MOOD TODAY:

☐ CHEERFUL   ☐ ANXIOUS   ☐ HOPEFUL
☐ CALM   ☐ TIRED   ☐ TENSE
☐ LIGHTHEARTED   ☐ MOTIVATED   ☐ BORED
☐ GLOOMY   ☐ LAZY   ☐ CONFIDENT
☐ STRESSED   ☐ REFLECTIVE   ☐ GRATEFUL
☐ ANGRY   ☐ ROMANTIC   ☐ OTHER: _____

FINAL THOUGHTS:

_____
_____
_____
_____

MORNING

GOAL: TODAY, I WILL SPEND _____ HOUR(S) OFF-SCREEN

DAILY OFF-SCREEN PLANNER

EXPLORE	MEET
TIME:	TIME:
MOVE	CREATE
TIME:	TIME:
LEARN	REFLECT
TIME:	TIME:
HELP	PLAY
TIME:	TIME:
PREP	OTHER
TIME:	TIME:

EVENING

TODAY I SPENT _____ HOUR(S) OFF-SCREEN.

WHAT I ENJOYED MOST FROM MY OFF-SCREEN TIME:
_____
_____
_____
_____
_____

CHALLENGES:
_____
_____
_____
_____
_____

MY OVERALL MOOD TODAY:

☐ CHEERFUL   ☐ ANXIOUS   ☐ HOPEFUL
☐ CALM   ☐ TIRED   ☐ TENSE
☐ LIGHTHEARTED   ☐ MOTIVATED   ☐ BORED
☐ GLOOMY   ☐ LAZY   ☐ CONFIDENT
☐ STRESSED   ☐ REFLECTIVE   ☐ GRATEFUL
☐ ANGRY   ☐ ROMANTIC   ☐ OTHER: _____

FINAL THOUGHTS:
_____
_____
_____
_____

MORNING

GOAL: TODAY, I WILL SPEND ____ HOUR(S) OFF-SCREEN

DAILY OFF-SCREEN PLANNER

EXPLORE	MEET
TIME:	TIME:
MOVE	CREATE
TIME:	TIME:
LEARN	REFLECT
TIME:	TIME:
HELP	PLAY
TIME:	TIME:
PREP	OTHER
TIME:	TIME:

EVENING

TODAY I SPENT _____ HOUR(S) OFF-SCREEN.

WHAT I ENJOYED MOST FROM MY OFF-SCREEN TIME:

_____
_____
_____
_____
_____

CHALLENGES:

_____
_____
_____
_____
_____

MY OVERALL MOOD TODAY:

☐ CHEERFUL   ☐ ANXIOUS   ☐ HOPEFUL
☐ CALM   ☐ TIRED   ☐ TENSE
☐ LIGHTHEARTED   ☐ MOTIVATED   ☐ BORED
☐ GLOOMY   ☐ LAZY   ☐ CONFIDENT
☐ STRESSED   ☐ REFLECTIVE   ☐ GRATEFUL
☐ ANGRY   ☐ ROMANTIC   ☐ OTHER: _____

FINAL THOUGHTS:

_____
_____
_____
_____

MORNING

GOAL: TODAY, I WILL SPEND _____ HOUR(S) OFF-SCREEN

DAILY OFF-SCREEN PLANNER

EXPLORE	MEET
TIME:	TIME:
MOVE	CREATE
TIME:	TIME:
LEARN	REFLECT
TIME:	TIME:
HELP	PLAY
TIME:	TIME:
PREP	OTHER
TIME:	TIME:

EVENING

TODAY I SPENT _____ HOUR(S) OFF-SCREEN.

WHAT I ENJOYED MOST FROM MY OFF-SCREEN TIME:

_____
_____
_____
_____
_____

CHALLENGES:

_____
_____
_____
_____
_____

MY OVERALL MOOD TODAY:

☐ CHEERFUL   ☐ ANXIOUS   ☐ HOPEFUL
☐ CALM   ☐ TIRED   ☐ TENSE
☐ LIGHTHEARTED ☐ MOTIVATED   ☐ BORED
☐ GLOOMY   ☐ LAZY   ☐ CONFIDENT
☐ STRESSED   ☐ REFLECTIVE   ☐ GRATEFUL
☐ ANGRY   ☐ ROMANTIC   ☐ OTHER: _____

FINAL THOUGHTS: _____

_____
_____
_____

MORNING

GOAL: TODAY, I WILL SPEND _____ HOUR(S) OFF-SCREEN

DAILY OFF-SCREEN PLANNER

EXPLORE	MEET
TIME:	TIME:
MOVE	CREATE
TIME:	TIME:
LEARN	REFLECT
TIME:	TIME:
HELP	PLAY
TIME:	TIME:
PREP	OTHER
TIME:	TIME:

EVENING

TODAY I SPENT _____ HOUR(S) OFF-SCREEN.

WHAT I ENJOYED MOST FROM MY OFF-SCREEN TIME:
_____
_____
_____
_____
_____

CHALLENGES:
_____
_____
_____
_____

MY OVERALL MOOD TODAY:

☐ CHEERFUL   ☐ ANXIOUS   ☐ HOPEFUL
☐ CALM   ☐ TIRED   ☐ TENSE
☐ LIGHTHEARTED   ☐ MOTIVATED   ☐ BORED
☐ GLOOMY   ☐ LAZY   ☐ CONFIDENT
☐ STRESSED   ☐ REFLECTIVE   ☐ GRATEFUL
☐ ANGRY   ☐ ROMANTIC   ☐ OTHER: _____

FINAL THOUGHTS:
_____
_____
_____
_____

MORNING

GOAL: TODAY, I WILL SPEND _____ HOUR(S) OFF-SCREEN

DAILY OFF-SCREEN PLANNER

EXPLORE	MEET
TIME:	TIME:
MOVE	CREATE
TIME:	TIME:
LEARN	REFLECT
TIME:	TIME:
HELP	PLAY
TIME:	TIME:
PREP	OTHER
TIME:	TIME:

EVENING

TODAY I SPENT _____ HOUR(S) OFF-SCREEN.

WHAT I ENJOYED MOST FROM MY OFF-SCREEN TIME:

_____
_____
_____
_____
_____

CHALLENGES:

_____
_____
_____
_____
_____

MY OVERALL MOOD TODAY:

☐ CHEERFUL   ☐ ANXIOUS   ☐ HOPEFUL
☐ CALM   ☐ TIRED   ☐ TENSE
☐ LIGHTHEARTED   ☐ MOTIVATED   ☐ BORED
☐ GLOOMY   ☐ LAZY   ☐ CONFIDENT
☐ STRESSED   ☐ REFLECTIVE   ☐ GRATEFUL
☐ ANGRY   ☐ ROMANTIC   ☐ OTHER: _____

FINAL THOUGHTS:

_____
_____
_____
_____

MORNING

GOAL: TODAY, I WILL SPEND _____ HOUR(S) OFF-SCREEN

DAILY OFF-SCREEN PLANNER

EXPLORE	MEET
TIME:	TIME:
MOVE	CREATE
TIME:	TIME:
LEARN	REFLECT
TIME:	TIME:
HELP	PLAY
TIME:	TIME:
PREP	OTHER
TIME:	TIME:

EVENING

TODAY I SPENT _____ HOUR(S) OFF-SCREEN.

WHAT I ENJOYED MOST FROM MY OFF-SCREEN TIME:

_____
_____
_____
_____
_____

CHALLENGES:

_____
_____
_____
_____
_____

MY OVERALL MOOD TODAY:

☐ CHEERFUL   ☐ ANXIOUS   ☐ HOPEFUL
☐ CALM   ☐ TIRED   ☐ TENSE
☐ LIGHTHEARTED   ☐ MOTIVATED   ☐ BORED
☐ GLOOMY   ☐ LAZY   ☐ CONFIDENT
☐ STRESSED   ☐ REFLECTIVE   ☐ GRATEFUL
☐ ANGRY   ☐ ROMANTIC   ☐ OTHER: _____

FINAL THOUGHTS:

_____
_____
_____
_____

MORNING

GOAL: TODAY, I WILL SPEND _____ HOUR(S) OFF-SCREEN

DAILY OFF-SCREEN PLANNER

EXPLORE	MEET
TIME:	TIME:
MOVE	CREATE
TIME:	TIME:
LEARN	REFLECT
TIME:	TIME:
HELP	PLAY
TIME:	TIME:
PREP	OTHER
TIME:	TIME:

EVENING

TODAY I SPENT _____ HOUR(S) OFF-SCREEN.

WHAT I ENJOYED MOST FROM MY OFF-SCREEN TIME:
_____
_____
_____
_____

CHALLENGES:
_____
_____
_____
_____

_____

MY OVERALL MOOD TODAY:

☐ CHEERFUL   ☐ ANXIOUS   ☐ HOPEFUL
☐ CALM   ☐ TIRED   ☐ TENSE
☐ LIGHTHEARTED   ☐ MOTIVATED   ☐ BORED
☐ GLOOMY   ☐ LAZY   ☐ CONFIDENT
☐ STRESSED   ☐ REFLECTIVE   ☐ GRATEFUL
☐ ANGRY   ☐ ROMANTIC   ☐ OTHER: _____

FINAL THOUGHTS:
_____
_____
_____
_____

MORNING

GOAL: TODAY, I WILL SPEND _____ HOUR(S) OFF-SCREEN

DAILY OFF-SCREEN PLANNER

EXPLORE	MEET
TIME:	TIME:
MOVE	CREATE
TIME:	TIME:
LEARN	REFLECT
TIME:	TIME:
HELP	PLAY
TIME:	TIME:
PREP	OTHER
TIME:	TIME:

EVENING

TODAY I SPENT _____ HOUR(S) OFF-SCREEN.

WHAT I ENJOYED MOST FROM MY OFF-SCREEN TIME:
_____
_____
_____
_____

CHALLENGES:
_____
_____
_____
_____

MY OVERALL MOOD TODAY:

☐ CHEERFUL   ☐ ANXIOUS   ☐ HOPEFUL
☐ CALM   ☐ TIRED   ☐ TENSE
☐ LIGHTHEARTED   ☐ MOTIVATED   ☐ BORED
☐ GLOOMY   ☐ LAZY   ☐ CONFIDENT
☐ STRESSED   ☐ REFLECTIVE   ☐ GRATEFUL
☐ ANGRY   ☐ ROMANTIC   ☐ OTHER: _____

FINAL THOUGHTS:
_____
_____
_____
_____

MORNING

GOAL: TODAY, I WILL SPEND _____ HOUR(S) OFF-SCREEN

DAILY OFF-SCREEN PLANNER

EXPLORE	MEET
TIME:	TIME:
MOVE	CREATE
TIME:	TIME:
LEARN	REFLECT
TIME:	TIME:
HELP	PLAY
TIME:	TIME:
PREP	OTHER
TIME:	TIME:

EVENING

TODAY I SPENT _____ HOUR(S) OFF-SCREEN.

WHAT I ENJOYED MOST FROM MY OFF-SCREEN TIME:

_____

_____

_____

_____

CHALLENGES:

_____

_____

_____

_____

MY OVERALL MOOD TODAY:

☐ CHEERFUL   ☐ ANXIOUS   ☐ HOPEFUL

☐ CALM   ☐ TIRED   ☐ TENSE

☐ LIGHTHEARTED   ☐ MOTIVATED   ☐ BORED

☐ GLOOMY   ☐ LAZY   ☐ CONFIDENT

☐ STRESSED   ☐ REFLECTIVE   ☐ GRATEFUL

☐ ANGRY   ☐ ROMANTIC   ☐ OTHER: _____

FINAL THOUGHTS:

_____

_____

_____

_____

MORNING

GOAL: TODAY, I WILL SPEND ____ HOUR(S) OFF-SCREEN

DAILY OFF-SCREEN PLANNER

EXPLORE	MEET
TIME:	TIME:
MOVE	CREATE
TIME:	TIME:
LEARN	REFLECT
TIME:	TIME:
HELP	PLAY
TIME:	TIME:
PREP	OTHER
TIME:	TIME:

EVENING

TODAY I SPENT _____ HOUR(S) OFF-SCREEN.

WHAT I ENJOYED MOST FROM MY OFF-SCREEN TIME:

_____

_____

_____

_____

CHALLENGES:

_____

_____

_____

MY OVERALL MOOD TODAY:

☐ CHEERFUL   ☐ ANXIOUS   ☐ HOPEFUL

☐ CALM   ☐ TIRED   ☐ TENSE

☐ LIGHTHEARTED   ☐ MOTIVATED   ☐ BORED

☐ GLOOMY   ☐ LAZY   ☐ CONFIDENT

☐ STRESSED   ☐ REFLECTIVE   ☐ GRATEFUL

☐ ANGRY   ☐ ROMANTIC   ☐ OTHER: _____

FINAL THOUGHTS:

_____

_____

_____

_____

MORNING

GOAL: TODAY, I WILL SPEND _____ HOUR(S) OFF-SCREEN

DAILY OFF-SCREEN PLANNER

EXPLORE	MEET
TIME:	TIME:
MOVE	CREATE
TIME:	TIME:
LEARN	REFLECT
TIME:	TIME:
HELP	PLAY
TIME:	TIME:
PREP	OTHER
TIME:	TIME:

EVENING

TODAY I SPENT _____ HOUR(S) OFF-SCREEN.

WHAT I ENJOYED MOST FROM MY OFF-SCREEN TIME:
_____
_____
_____
_____

CHALLENGES:
_____
_____
_____
_____

MY OVERALL MOOD TODAY:

- ☐ CHEERFUL
- ☐ CALM
- ☐ LIGHTHEARTED
- ☐ GLOOMY
- ☐ STRESSED
- ☐ ANGRY

- ☐ ANXIOUS
- ☐ TIRED
- ☐ MOTIVATED
- ☐ LAZY
- ☐ REFLECTIVE
- ☐ ROMANTIC

- ☐ HOPEFUL
- ☐ TENSE
- ☐ BORED
- ☐ CONFIDENT
- ☐ GRATEFUL
- ☐ OTHER: _____

FINAL THOUGHTS:
_____
_____
_____
_____

MORNING

GOAL: TODAY, I WILL SPEND _____ HOUR(S) OFF-SCREEN

DAILY OFF-SCREEN PLANNER

EXPLORE TIME:	MEET TIME:
MOVE TIME:	CREATE TIME:
LEARN· TIME:	REFLECT TIME:
HELP TIME:	PLAY TIME:
PREP TIME:	OTHER TIME:

EVENING

TODAY I SPENT _____ HOUR(S) OFF-SCREEN.

WHAT I ENJOYED MOST FROM MY OFF-SCREEN TIME:

_____

_____

_____

_____

CHALLENGES:

_____

_____

_____

_____

MY OVERALL MOOD TODAY:

- [ ] CHEERFUL
- [ ] CALM
- [ ] LIGHTHEARTED
- [ ] GLOOMY
- [ ] STRESSED
- [ ] ANGRY

- [ ] ANXIOUS
- [ ] TIRED
- [ ] MOTIVATED
- [ ] LAZY
- [ ] REFLECTIVE
- [ ] ROMANTIC

- [ ] HOPEFUL
- [ ] TENSE
- [ ] BORED
- [ ] CONFIDENT
- [ ] GRATEFUL
- [ ] OTHER: _____

FINAL THOUGHTS:

_____

_____

_____

_____

MORNING

GOAL: TODAY, I WILL SPEND _____ HOUR(S) OFF-SCREEN

DAILY OFF-SCREEN PLANNER

EXPLORE	MEET
TIME:	TIME:
MOVE	CREATE
TIME:	TIME:
LEARN	REFLECT
TIME:	TIME:
HELP	PLAY
TIME:	TIME:
PREP	OTHER
TIME:	TIME:

EVENING

TODAY I SPENT _____ HOUR(S) OFF-SCREEN.

WHAT I ENJOYED MOST FROM MY OFF-SCREEN TIME:
_____
_____
_____
_____

CHALLENGES:
_____
_____
_____
_____

MY OVERALL MOOD TODAY:

☐ CHEERFUL   ☐ ANXIOUS   ☐ HOPEFUL
☐ CALM   ☐ TIRED   ☐ TENSE
☐ LIGHTHEARTED   ☐ MOTIVATED   ☐ BORED
☐ GLOOMY   ☐ LAZY   ☐ CONFIDENT
☐ STRESSED   ☐ REFLECTIVE   ☐ GRATEFUL
☐ ANGRY   ☐ ROMANTIC   ☐ OTHER: _____

FINAL THOUGHTS: _____
_____
_____
_____
_____

MORNING

GOAL: TODAY, I WILL SPEND _____ HOUR(S) OFF-SCREEN

DAILY OFF-SCREEN PLANNER

EXPLORE	MEET
TIME:	TIME:
MOVE	CREATE
TIME:	TIME:
LEARN	REFLECT
TIME:	TIME:
HELP	PLAY
TIME:	TIME:
PREP	OTHER
TIME:	TIME:

EVENING

TODAY I SPENT _____ HOUR(S) OFF-SCREEN.

WHAT I ENJOYED MOST FROM MY OFF-SCREEN TIME:

_____

_____

_____

_____

CHALLENGES:

_____

_____

_____

_____

MY OVERALL MOOD TODAY:

☐ CHEERFUL   ☐ ANXIOUS   ☐ HOPEFUL

☐ CALM   ☐ TIRED   ☐ TENSE

☐ LIGHTHEARTED   ☐ MOTIVATED   ☐ BORED

☐ GLOOMY   ☐ LAZY   ☐ CONFIDENT

☐ STRESSED   ☐ REFLECTIVE   ☐ GRATEFUL

☐ ANGRY   ☐ ROMANTIC   ☐ OTHER: _____

FINAL THOUGHTS:

_____

_____

_____

_____

MORNING

GOAL: TODAY, I WILL SPEND _____ HOUR(S) OFF-SCREEN

DAILY OFF-SCREEN PLANNER

EXPLORE	MEET
TIME:	TIME:
MOVE	CREATE
TIME:	TIME:
LEARN	REFLECT
TIME:	TIME:
HELP	PLAY
TIME:	TIME:
PREP	OTHER
TIME:	TIME:

EVENING

TODAY I SPENT _____ HOUR(S) OFF-SCREEN.

WHAT I ENJOYED MOST FROM MY OFF-SCREEN TIME:

_____
_____
_____
_____

CHALLENGES:

_____
_____
_____

MY OVERALL MOOD TODAY:

☐ CHEERFUL   ☐ ANXIOUS   ☐ HOPEFUL
☐ CALM   ☐ TIRED   ☐ TENSE
☐ LIGHTHEARTED ☐ MOTIVATED   ☐ BORED
☐ GLOOMY   ☐ LAZY   ☐ CONFIDENT
☐ STRESSED   ☐ REFLECTIVE   ☐ GRATEFUL
☐ ANGRY   ☐ ROMANTIC   ☐ OTHER: _____

FINAL THOUGHTS:

_____
_____
_____
_____

MORNING

GOAL: TODAY, I WILL SPEND _____ HOUR(S) OFF-SCREEN

DAILY OFF-SCREEN PLANNER

EXPLORE	MEET
TIME:	TIME:
MOVE	CREATE
TIME:	TIME:
LEARN	REFLECT
TIME:	TIME:
HELP	PLAY
TIME:	TIME:
PREP	OTHER
TIME:	TIME:

EVENING

TODAY I SPENT _____ HOUR(S) OFF-SCREEN.

WHAT I ENJOYED MOST FROM MY OFF-SCREEN TIME:

_____
_____
_____
_____

CHALLENGES:

_____
_____
_____
_____

MY OVERALL MOOD TODAY:

- [ ] CHEERFUL
- [ ] CALM
- [ ] LIGHTHEARTED
- [ ] GLOOMY
- [ ] STRESSED
- [ ] ANGRY

- [ ] ANXIOUS
- [ ] TIRED
- [ ] MOTIVATED
- [ ] LAZY
- [ ] REFLECTIVE
- [ ] ROMANTIC

- [ ] HOPEFUL
- [ ] TENSE
- [ ] BORED
- [ ] CONFIDENT
- [ ] GRATEFUL
- [ ] OTHER: _____

FINAL THOUGHTS:

_____
_____
_____
_____
_____

MORNING

GOAL: TODAY, I WILL SPEND _____ HOUR(S) OFF-SCREEN

DAILY OFF-SCREEN PLANNER

EXPLORE	MEET
TIME:	TIME:
MOVE	CREATE
TIME:	TIME:
LEARN	REFLECT
TIME:	TIME:
HELP	PLAY
TIME:	TIME:
PREP	OTHER
TIME:	TIME:

EVENING

TODAY I SPENT _____ HOUR(S) OFF-SCREEN.

WHAT I ENJOYED MOST FROM MY OFF-SCREEN TIME:

_____
_____
_____
_____

CHALLENGES:

_____
_____
_____
_____

MY OVERALL MOOD TODAY:

☐ CHEERFUL   ☐ ANXIOUS   ☐ HOPEFUL
☐ CALM   ☐ TIRED   ☐ TENSE
☐ LIGHTHEARTED ☐ MOTIVATED   ☐ BORED
☐ GLOOMY   ☐ LAZY   ☐ CONFIDENT
☐ STRESSED   ☐ REFLECTIVE   ☐ GRATEFUL
☐ ANGRY   ☐ ROMANTIC   ☐ OTHER: _____

FINAL THOUGHTS:

_____
_____
_____
_____

MORNING

GOAL: TODAY, I WILL SPEND _____ HOUR(S) OFF-SCREEN

DAILY OFF-SCREEN PLANNER

EXPLORE	MEET
TIME:	TIME:
MOVE	CREATE
TIME:	TIME:
LEARN	REFLECT
TIME:	TIME:
HELP	PLAY
TIME:	TIME:
PREP	OTHER
TIME:	TIME:

EVENING

TODAY I SPENT _____ HOUR(S) OFF-SCREEN.

WHAT I ENJOYED MOST FROM MY OFF-SCREEN TIME:

_____

_____

_____

_____

CHALLENGES:

_____

_____

_____

_____

MY OVERALL MOOD TODAY:

☐ CHEERFUL   ☐ ANXIOUS   ☐ HOPEFUL
☐ CALM   ☐ TIRED   ☐ TENSE
☐ LIGHTHEARTED   ☐ MOTIVATED   ☐ BORED
☐ GLOOMY   ☐ LAZY   ☐ CONFIDENT
☐ STRESSED   ☐ REFLECTIVE   ☐ GRATEFUL
☐ ANGRY   ☐ ROMANTIC   ☐ OTHER: _____

FINAL THOUGHTS:

_____

_____

_____

_____

MORNING

GOAL: TODAY, I WILL SPEND _____ HOUR(S) OFF-SCREE

DAILY OFF-SCREEN PLANNER

EXPLORE	MEET
TIME:	TIME:
MOVE	CREATE
TIME:	TIME:
LEARN	REFLECT
TIME:	TIME:
HELP	PLAY
TIME:	TIME:
PREP	OTHER
TIME:	TIME:

EVENING

TODAY I SPENT _____ HOUR(S) OFF-SCREEN.

WHAT I ENJOYED MOST FROM MY OFF-SCREEN TIME:

_____

_____

_____

_____

CHALLENGES:

_____

_____

_____

_____

MY OVERALL MOOD TODAY:

- [ ] CHEERFUL
- [ ] CALM
- [ ] LIGHTHEARTED
- [ ] GLOOMY
- [ ] STRESSED
- [ ] ANGRY

- [ ] ANXIOUS
- [ ] TIRED
- [ ] MOTIVATED
- [ ] LAZY
- [ ] REFLECTIVE
- [ ] ROMANTIC

- [ ] HOPEFUL
- [ ] TENSE
- [ ] BORED
- [ ] CONFIDENT
- [ ] GRATEFUL
- [ ] OTHER: _____

FINAL THOUGHTS:

_____

_____

_____

_____

MORNING

GOAL: TODAY, I WILL SPEND _____ HOUR(S) OFF-SCREEN

DAILY OFF-SCREEN PLANNER

EXPLORE	MEET
TIME:	TIME:
MOVE	CREATE
TIME:	TIME:
LEARN	REFLECT
TIME:	TIME:
HELP	PLAY
TIME:	TIME:
PREP	OTHER
TIME:	TIME:

EVENING

TODAY I SPENT _____ HOUR(S) OFF-SCREEN.

WHAT I ENJOYED MOST FROM MY OFF-SCREEN TIME:
_____
_____
_____
_____
_____

CHALLENGES:
_____
_____
_____
_____

MY OVERALL MOOD TODAY:

- [ ] CHEERFUL
- [ ] CALM
- [ ] LIGHTHEARTED
- [ ] GLOOMY
- [ ] STRESSED
- [ ] ANGRY

- [ ] ANXIOUS
- [ ] TIRED
- [ ] MOTIVATED
- [ ] LAZY
- [ ] REFLECTIVE
- [ ] ROMANTIC

- [ ] HOPEFUL
- [ ] TENSE
- [ ] BORED
- [ ] CONFIDENT
- [ ] GRATEFUL
- [ ] OTHER: _____

FINAL THOUGHTS:
_____
_____
_____
_____

MORNING

GOAL: TODAY, I WILL SPEND _____ HOUR(S) OFF-SCREEN

DAILY OFF-SCREEN PLANNER

EXPLORE	MEET
TIME:	TIME:
MOVE	CREATE
TIME:	TIME:
LEARN	REFLECT
TIME:	TIME:
HELP	PLAY
TIME:	TIME:
PREP	OTHER
TIME:	TIME:

EVENING

TODAY I SPENT _____ HOUR(S) OFF-SCREEN.

WHAT I ENJOYED MOST FROM MY OFF-SCREEN TIME:
_____
_____
_____
_____
_____

CHALLENGES:
_____
_____
_____
_____

MY OVERALL MOOD TODAY:

☐ CHEERFUL   ☐ ANXIOUS   ☐ HOPEFUL
☐ CALM   ☐ TIRED   ☐ TENSE
☐ LIGHTHEARTED   ☐ MOTIVATED   ☐ BORED
☐ GLOOMY   ☐ LAZY   ☐ CONFIDENT
☐ STRESSED   ☐ REFLECTIVE   ☐ GRATEFUL
☐ ANGRY   ☐ ROMANTIC   ☐ OTHER: _____

FINAL THOUGHTS:
_____
_____
_____
_____

MORNING

GOAL: TODAY, I WILL SPEND _____ HOUR(S) OFF-SCREEN

DAILY OFF-SCREEN PLANNER

EXPLORE	MEET
TIME:	TIME:
MOVE	CREATE
TIME:	TIME:
LEARN	REFLECT
TIME:	TIME:
HELP	PLAY
TIME:	TIME:
PREP	OTHER
TIME:	TIME:

EVENING

TODAY I SPENT _____ HOUR(S) OFF-SCREEN.

WHAT I ENJOYED MOST FROM MY OFF-SCREEN TIME:
_____
_____
_____
_____
_____

CHALLENGES:
_____
_____
_____
_____
_____

MY OVERALL MOOD TODAY:

☐ CHEERFUL   ☐ ANXIOUS   ☐ HOPEFUL
☐ CALM   ☐ TIRED   ☐ TENSE
☐ LIGHTHEARTED   ☐ MOTIVATED   ☐ BORED
☐ GLOOMY   ☐ LAZY   ☐ CONFIDENT
☐ STRESSED   ☐ REFLECTIVE   ☐ GRATEFUL
☐ ANGRY   ☐ ROMANTIC   ☐ OTHER: _____

FINAL THOUGHTS:
_____
_____
_____
_____
_____

MORNING

GOAL: TODAY, I WILL SPEND _____ HOUR(S) OFF-SCREEN

DAILY OFF-SCREEN PLANNER

EXPLORE	MEET
TIME:	TIME:
MOVE	CREATE
TIME:	TIME:
LEARN	REFLECT
TIME:	TIME:
HELP	PLAY
TIME:	TIME:
PREP	OTHER
TIME:	TIME:

EVENING

TODAY I SPENT _____ HOUR(S) OFF-SCREEN.

WHAT I ENJOYED MOST FROM MY OFF-SCREEN TIME:

_____
_____
_____
_____
_____

CHALLENGES:

_____
_____
_____
_____
_____

MY OVERALL MOOD TODAY:

☐ CHEERFUL   ☐ ANXIOUS   ☐ HOPEFUL
☐ CALM   ☐ TIRED   ☐ TENSE
☐ LIGHTHEARTED   ☐ MOTIVATED   ☐ BORED
☐ GLOOMY   ☐ LAZY   ☐ CONFIDENT
☐ STRESSED   ☐ REFLECTIVE   ☐ GRATEFUL
☐ ANGRY   ☐ ROMANTIC   ☐ OTHER: _____

FINAL THOUGHTS:

_____
_____
_____
_____
_____

MORNING

GOAL: TODAY, I WILL SPEND _____ HOUR(S) OFF-SCREEN

DAILY OFF-SCREEN PLANNER

EXPLORE	MEET
TIME:	TIME:
MOVE	CREATE
TIME:	TIME:
LEARN	REFLECT
TIME:	TIME:
HELP	PLAY
TIME:	TIME:
PREP	OTHER
TIME:	TIME:

EVENING

TODAY I SPENT _____ HOUR(S) OFF-SCREEN.

WHAT I ENJOYED MOST FROM MY OFF-SCREEN TIME:
_____
_____
_____
_____

CHALLENGES:
_____
_____
_____
_____

MY OVERALL MOOD TODAY:

☐ CHEERFUL ☐ ANXIOUS ☐ HOPEFUL
☐ CALM ☐ TIRED ☐ TENSE
☐ LIGHTHEARTED ☐ MOTIVATED ☐ BORED
☐ GLOOMY ☐ LAZY ☐ CONFIDENT
☐ STRESSED ☐ REFLECTIVE ☐ GRATEFUL
☐ ANGRY ☐ ROMANTIC ☐ OTHER: _____

FINAL THOUGHTS:
_____
_____
_____
_____

MORNING

GOAL: TODAY, I WILL SPEND _____ HOUR(S) OFF-SCREEN

DAILY OFF-SCREEN PLANNER

EXPLORE	MEET
TIME:	TIME:
MOVE	CREATE
TIME:	TIME:
LEARN	REFLECT
TIME:	TIME:
HELP	PLAY
TIME:	TIME:
PREP	OTHER
TIME:	TIME:

EVENING

TODAY I SPENT _____ HOUR(S) OFF-SCREEN.

WHAT I ENJOYED MOST FROM MY OFF-SCREEN TIME:
_____
_____
_____
_____
_____

CHALLENGES:
_____
_____
_____
_____

MY OVERALL MOOD TODAY:

☐ CHEERFUL   ☐ ANXIOUS   ☐ HOPEFUL

☐ CALM   ☐ TIRED   ☐ TENSE

☐ LIGHTHEARTED   ☐ MOTIVATED   ☐ BORED

☐ GLOOMY   ☐ LAZY   ☐ CONFIDENT

☐ STRESSED   ☐ REFLECTIVE   ☐ GRATEFUL

☐ ANGRY   ☐ ROMANTIC   ☐ OTHER: _____

FINAL THOUGHTS:
_____
_____
_____
_____

MORNING

GOAL: TODAY, I WILL SPEND _____ HOUR(S) OFF-SCREEN

DAILY OFF-SCREEN PLANNER

EXPLORE	MEET
TIME:	TIME:
MOVE	CREATE
TIME:	TIME:
LEARN	REFLECT
TIME:	TIME:
HELP	PLAY
TIME:	TIME:
PREP	OTHER
TIME:	TIME:

EVENING

TODAY I SPENT _____ HOUR(S) OFF-SCREEN.

WHAT I ENJOYED MOST FROM MY OFF-SCREEN TIME:

_____
_____
_____
_____
_____

CHALLENGES:

_____
_____
_____
_____

MY OVERALL MOOD TODAY:

☐ CHEERFUL   ☐ ANXIOUS   ☐ HOPEFUL
☐ CALM   ☐ TIRED   ☐ TENSE
☐ LIGHTHEARTED   ☐ MOTIVATED   ☐ BORED
☐ GLOOMY   ☐ LAZY   ☐ CONFIDENT
☐ STRESSED   ☐ REFLECTIVE   ☐ GRATEFUL
☐ ANGRY   ☐ ROMANTIC   ☐ OTHER: _____

FINAL THOUGHTS:

_____
_____
_____
_____
_____

MORNING

GOAL: TODAY, I WILL SPEND _____ HOUR(S) OFF-SCREE

DAILY OFF-SCREEN PLANNER

EXPLORE	MEET
TIME:	TIME:
MOVE	CREATE
TIME:	TIME:
LEARN	REFLECT
TIME:	TIME:
HELP	PLAY
TIME:	TIME:
PREP	OTHER
TIME:	TIME:

EVENING

TODAY I SPENT _____ HOUR(S) OFF-SCREEN.

WHAT I ENJOYED MOST FROM MY OFF-SCREEN TIME:

_____

_____

_____

_____

_____

CHALLENGES:

_____

_____

_____

_____

MY OVERALL MOOD TODAY:

☐ CHEERFUL   ☐ ANXIOUS   ☐ HOPEFUL

☐ CALM   ☐ TIRED   ☐ TENSE

☐ LIGHTHEARTED   ☐ MOTIVATED   ☐ BORED

☐ GLOOMY   ☐ LAZY   ☐ CONFIDENT

☐ STRESSED   ☐ REFLECTIVE   ☐ GRATEFUL

☐ ANGRY   ☐ ROMANTIC   ☐ OTHER: _____

FINAL THOUGHTS:

_____

_____

_____

_____

MORNING

GOAL: TODAY, I WILL SPEND _____ HOUR(S) OFF-SCREEN

DAILY OFF-SCREEN PLANNER

EXPLORE	MEET
TIME:	TIME:
MOVE	CREATE
TIME:	TIME:
LEARN	REFLECT
TIME:	TIME:
HELP	PLAY
TIME:	TIME:
PREP	OTHER
TIME:	TIME:

EVENING

TODAY I SPENT _____ HOUR(S) OFF-SCREEN.

WHAT I ENJOYED MOST FROM MY OFF-SCREEN TIME:
_____
_____
_____
_____
_____

CHALLENGES: _____
_____
_____
_____
_____

MY OVERALL MOOD TODAY:

☐ CHEERFUL   ☐ ANXIOUS   ☐ HOPEFUL
☐ CALM   ☐ TIRED   ☐ TENSE
☐ LIGHTHEARTED   ☐ MOTIVATED   ☐ BORED
☐ GLOOMY   ☐ LAZY   ☐ CONFIDENT
☐ STRESSED   ☐ REFLECTIVE   ☐ GRATEFUL
☐ ANGRY   ☐ ROMANTIC   ☐ OTHER: _____

FINAL THOUGHTS: _____
_____
_____
_____
_____

MORNING

GOAL: TODAY, I WILL SPEND _____ HOUR(S) OFF-SCREE

DAILY OFF-SCREEN PLANNER

EXPLORE	MEET
TIME:	TIME:
MOVE	CREATE
TIME:	TIME:
LEARN	REFLECT
TIME:	TIME:
HELP	PLAY
TIME:	TIME:
PREP	OTHER
TIME:	TIME:

EVENING

TODAY I SPENT _____ HOUR(S) OFF-SCREEN.

WHAT I ENJOYED MOST FROM MY OFF-SCREEN TIME:
_____
_____
_____
_____
_____

CHALLENGES:
_____
_____
_____
_____

MY OVERALL MOOD TODAY:

☐ CHEERFUL   ☐ ANXIOUS   ☐ HOPEFUL

☐ CALM   ☐ TIRED   ☐ TENSE

☐ LIGHTHEARTED   ☐ MOTIVATED   ☐ BORED

☐ GLOOMY   ☐ LAZY   ☐ CONFIDENT

☐ STRESSED   ☐ REFLECTIVE   ☐ GRATEFUL

☐ ANGRY   ☐ ROMANTIC   ☐ OTHER: _____

FINAL THOUGHTS:
_____
_____
_____
_____
_____

MORNING

GOAL: TODAY, I WILL SPEND _____ HOUR(S) OFF-SCREE

DAILY OFF-SCREEN PLANNER

EXPLORE	MEET
TIME:	TIME:
MOVE	CREATE
TIME:	TIME:
LEARN	REFLECT
TIME:	TIME:
HELP	PLAY
TIME:	TIME:
PREP	OTHER
TIME:	TIME:

EVENING

TODAY I SPENT _____ HOUR(S) OFF-SCREEN.

WHAT I ENJOYED MOST FROM MY OFF-SCREEN TIME:
_____
_____
_____
_____
_____

CHALLENGES:
_____
_____
_____
_____

MY OVERALL MOOD TODAY:

☐ CHEERFUL   ☐ ANXIOUS   ☐ HOPEFUL

☐ CALM   ☐ TIRED   ☐ TENSE

☐ LIGHTHEARTED   ☐ MOTIVATED   ☐ BORED

☐ GLOOMY   ☐ LAZY   ☐ CONFIDENT

☐ STRESSED   ☐ REFLECTIVE   ☐ GRATEFUL

☐ ANGRY   ☐ ROMANTIC   ☐ OTHER: _____

FINAL THOUGHTS:
_____
_____
_____
_____

MORNING

GOAL: TODAY, I WILL SPEND _____ HOUR(S) OFF-SCREEN

DAILY OFF-SCREEN PLANNER

EXPLORE	MEET
TIME:	TIME:
MOVE	CREATE
TIME:	TIME:
LEARN	REFLECT
TIME:	TIME:
HELP	PLAY
TIME:	TIME:
PREP	OTHER
TIME:	TIME:

EVENING

TODAY I SPENT _____ HOUR(S) OFF-SCREEN.

WHAT I ENJOYED MOST FROM MY OFF-SCREEN TIME:

_____
_____
_____
_____
_____

CHALLENGES:

_____
_____
_____
_____

MY OVERALL MOOD TODAY:

☐ CHEERFUL   ☐ ANXIOUS   ☐ HOPEFUL
☐ CALM   ☐ TIRED   ☐ TENSE
☐ LIGHTHEARTED   ☐ MOTIVATED   ☐ BORED
☐ GLOOMY   ☐ LAZY   ☐ CONFIDENT
☐ STRESSED   ☐ REFLECTIVE   ☐ GRATEFUL
☐ ANGRY   ☐ ROMANTIC   ☐ OTHER: _____

FINAL THOUGHTS:

_____
_____
_____
_____
_____

MORNING

GOAL: TODAY, I WILL SPEND _____ HOUR(S) OFF-SCREEI

DAILY OFF-SCREEN PLANNER

EXPLORE	MEET
TIME:	TIME:
MOVE	CREATE
TIME:	TIME:
LEARN	REFLECT
TIME:	TIME:
HELP	PLAY
TIME:	TIME:
PREP	OTHER
TIME:	TIME:

EVENING

TODAY I SPENT _____ HOUR(S) OFF-SCREEN.

WHAT I ENJOYED MOST FROM MY OFF-SCREEN TIME:

_____
_____
_____
_____
_____

CHALLENGES:

_____
_____
_____
_____

MY OVERALL MOOD TODAY:

☐ CHEERFUL   ☐ ANXIOUS   ☐ HOPEFUL
☐ CALM   ☐ TIRED   ☐ TENSE
☐ LIGHTHEARTED   ☐ MOTIVATED   ☐ BORED
☐ GLOOMY   ☐ LAZY   ☐ CONFIDENT
☐ STRESSED   ☐ REFLECTIVE   ☐ GRATEFUL
☐ ANGRY   ☐ ROMANTIC   ☐ OTHER: _____

FINAL THOUGHTS:

_____
_____
_____
_____

MORNING

GOAL: TODAY, I WILL SPEND _____ HOUR(S) OFF-SCREEN

DAILY OFF-SCREEN PLANNER

EXPLORE	MEET
TIME:	TIME:
MOVE	CREATE
TIME:	TIME:
LEARN	REFLECT
TIME:	TIME:
HELP	PLAY
TIME:	TIME:
PREP	OTHER
TIME:	TIME:

EVENING

TODAY I SPENT _____ HOUR(S) OFF-SCREEN.

WHAT I ENJOYED MOST FROM MY OFF-SCREEN TIME:

_____
_____
_____
_____
_____

CHALLENGES:

_____
_____
_____
_____

MY OVERALL MOOD TODAY:

☐ CHEERFUL   ☐ ANXIOUS   ☐ HOPEFUL
☐ CALM   ☐ TIRED   ☐ TENSE
☐ LIGHTHEARTED ☐ MOTIVATED   ☐ BORED
☐ GLOOMY   ☐ LAZY   ☐ CONFIDENT
☐ STRESSED   ☐ REFLECTIVE   ☐ GRATEFUL
☐ ANGRY   ☐ ROMANTIC   ☐ OTHER: _____

FINAL THOUGHTS:

_____
_____
_____
_____
_____

MORNING

GOAL: TODAY, I WILL SPEND _____ HOUR(S) OFF-SCREEN

DAILY OFF-SCREEN PLANNER

EXPLORE	MEET
TIME:	TIME:
MOVE	CREATE
TIME:	TIME:
LEARN	REFLECT
TIME:	TIME:
HELP	PLAY
TIME:	TIME:
PREP	OTHER
TIME:	TIME:

EVENING

TODAY I SPENT _____ HOUR(S) OFF-SCREEN.

WHAT I ENJOYED MOST FROM MY OFF-SCREEN TIME:

_____

_____

_____

_____

CHALLENGES: _____

_____

_____

_____

_____

MY OVERALL MOOD TODAY:

☐ CHEERFUL   ☐ ANXIOUS   ☐ HOPEFUL
☐ CALM   ☐ TIRED   ☐ TENSE
☐ LIGHTHEARTED   ☐ MOTIVATED   ☐ BORED
☐ GLOOMY   ☐ LAZY   ☐ CONFIDENT
☐ STRESSED   ☐ REFLECTIVE   ☐ GRATEFUL
☐ ANGRY   ☐ ROMANTIC   ☐ OTHER: _____

FINAL THOUGHTS: _____

_____

_____

_____

_____

MORNING

GOAL: TODAY, I WILL SPEND _____ HOUR(S) OFF-SCREEN

DAILY OFF-SCREEN PLANNER

EXPLORE	MEET
TIME:	TIME:
MOVE	CREATE
TIME:	TIME:
LEARN	REFLECT
TIME:	TIME:
HELP	PLAY
TIME:	TIME:
PREP	OTHER
TIME:	TIME:

EVENING

TODAY I SPENT _____ HOUR(S) OFF-SCREEN.

WHAT I ENJOYED MOST FROM MY OFF-SCREEN TIME:

_____

_____

_____

_____

CHALLENGES:

_____

_____

_____

MY OVERALL MOOD TODAY:

- ☐ CHEERFUL
- ☐ CALM
- ☐ LIGHTHEARTED
- ☐ GLOOMY
- ☐ STRESSED
- ☐ ANGRY

- ☐ ANXIOUS
- ☐ TIRED
- ☐ MOTIVATED
- ☐ LAZY
- ☐ REFLECTIVE
- ☐ ROMANTIC

- ☐ HOPEFUL
- ☐ TENSE
- ☐ BORED
- ☐ CONFIDENT
- ☐ GRATEFUL
- ☐ OTHER: _____

FINAL THOUGHTS:

_____

_____

_____

_____

MORNING

GOAL: TODAY, I WILL SPEND _____ HOUR(S) OFF-SCREE

DAILY OFF-SCREEN PLANNER

EXPLORE	MEET
TIME:	TIME:
MOVE	CREATE
TIME:	TIME:
LEARN	REFLECT
TIME:	TIME:
HELP	PLAY
TIME:	TIME:
PREP	OTHER
TIME:	TIME:

EVENING

TODAY I SPENT _____ HOUR(S) OFF-SCREEN.

WHAT I ENJOYED MOST FROM MY OFF-SCREEN TIME:

_____
_____
_____
_____

CHALLENGES:

_____
_____
_____
_____

MY OVERALL MOOD TODAY:

☐ CHEERFUL   ☐ ANXIOUS   ☐ HOPEFUL
☐ CALM   ☐ TIRED   ☐ TENSE
☐ LIGHTHEARTED   ☐ MOTIVATED   ☐ BORED
☐ GLOOMY   ☐ LAZY   ☐ CONFIDENT
☐ STRESSED   ☐ REFLECTIVE   ☐ GRATEFUL
☐ ANGRY   ☐ ROMANTIC   ☐ OTHER: _____

FINAL THOUGHTS:

_____
_____
_____
_____
_____

MORNING

GOAL: TODAY, I WILL SPEND _____ HOUR(S) OFF-SCREE

DAILY OFF-SCREEN PLANNER

EXPLORE	MEET
TIME:	TIME:
MOVE	CREATE
TIME:	TIME:
LEARN	REFLECT
TIME:	TIME:
HELP	PLAY
TIME:	TIME:
PREP	OTHER
TIME:	TIME:

EVENING

TODAY I SPENT _____ HOUR(S) OFF-SCREEN.

WHAT I ENJOYED MOST FROM MY OFF-SCREEN TIME:

_____

_____

_____

_____

CHALLENGES:

_____

_____

_____

MY OVERALL MOOD TODAY:

☐ CHEERFUL   ☐ ANXIOUS   ☐ HOPEFUL

☐ CALM   ☐ TIRED   ☐ TENSE

☐ LIGHTHEARTED   ☐ MOTIVATED   ☐ BORED

☐ GLOOMY   ☐ LAZY   ☐ CONFIDENT

☐ STRESSED   ☐ REFLECTIVE   ☐ GRATEFUL

☐ ANGRY   ☐ ROMANTIC   ☐ OTHER: _____

FINAL THOUGHTS:

_____

_____

_____

_____

MORNING

GOAL: TODAY, I WILL SPEND _____ HOUR(S) OFF-SCREE

DAILY OFF-SCREEN PLANNER

EXPLORE	MEET
TIME:	TIME:
MOVE	CREATE
TIME:	TIME:
LEARN	REFLECT
TIME:	TIME:
HELP	PLAY
TIME:	TIME:
PREP	OTHER
TIME:	TIME:

EVENING

TODAY I SPENT _____ HOUR(S) OFF-SCREEN.

WHAT I ENJOYED MOST FROM MY OFF-SCREEN TIME:
_____
_____
_____
_____

CHALLENGES:
_____
_____
_____
_____

MY OVERALL MOOD TODAY:

☐ CHEERFUL   ☐ ANXIOUS   ☐ HOPEFUL
☐ CALM   ☐ TIRED   ☐ TENSE
☐ LIGHTHEARTED   ☐ MOTIVATED   ☐ BORED
☐ GLOOMY   ☐ LAZY   ☐ CONFIDENT
☐ STRESSED   ☐ REFLECTIVE   ☐ GRATEFUL
☐ ANGRY   ☐ ROMANTIC   ☐ OTHER: _____

FINAL THOUGHTS:
_____
_____
_____
_____
_____

MORNING

GOAL: TODAY, I WILL SPEND _____ HOUR(S) OFF-SCREEN

DAILY OFF-SCREEN PLANNER

EXPLORE TIME:	MEET TIME:
MOVE TIME:	CREATE TIME:
LEARN TIME:	REFLECT TIME:
HELP TIME:	PLAY TIME:
PREP TIME:	OTHER TIME:

EVENING

TODAY I SPENT _____ HOUR(S) OFF-SCREEN.

WHAT I ENJOYED MOST FROM MY OFF-SCREEN TIME:

_____
_____
_____
_____

CHALLENGES:

_____
_____
_____
_____

MY OVERALL MOOD TODAY:

☐ CHEERFUL   ☐ ANXIOUS   ☐ HOPEFUL

☐ CALM   ☐ TIRED   ☐ TENSE

☐ LIGHTHEARTED   ☐ MOTIVATED   ☐ BORED

☐ GLOOMY   ☐ LAZY   ☐ CONFIDENT

☐ STRESSED   ☐ REFLECTIVE   ☐ GRATEFUL

☐ ANGRY   ☐ ROMANTIC   ☐ OTHER: _____

FINAL THOUGHTS:

_____
_____
_____
_____

MORNING

GOAL: TODAY, I WILL SPEND _____ HOUR(S) OFF-SCREEN

DAILY OFF-SCREEN PLANNER

EXPLORE	MEET
TIME:	TIME:
MOVE	CREATE
TIME:	TIME:
LEARN	REFLECT
TIME:	TIME:
HELP	PLAY
TIME:	TIME:
PREP	OTHER
TIME:	TIME:

EVENING

TODAY I SPENT _____ HOUR(S) OFF-SCREEN.

WHAT I ENJOYED MOST FROM MY OFF-SCREEN TIME:

_____
_____
_____
_____

CHALLENGES:

_____
_____
_____
_____

MY OVERALL MOOD TODAY:

☐ CHEERFUL   ☐ ANXIOUS   ☐ HOPEFUL
☐ CALM   ☐ TIRED   ☐ TENSE
☐ LIGHTHEARTED   ☐ MOTIVATED   ☐ BORED
☐ GLOOMY   ☐ LAZY   ☐ CONFIDENT
☐ STRESSED   ☐ REFLECTIVE   ☐ GRATEFUL
☐ ANGRY   ☐ ROMANTIC   ☐ OTHER: _____

FINAL THOUGHTS:

_____
_____
_____
_____
_____

MORNING

GOAL: TODAY, I WILL SPEND _____ HOUR(S) OFF-SCREEN

DAILY OFF-SCREEN PLANNER

EXPLORE	MEET
TIME:	TIME:
MOVE	CREATE
TIME:	TIME:
LEARN	REFLECT
TIME:	TIME:
HELP	PLAY
TIME:	TIME:
PREP	OTHER
TIME:	TIME:

EVENING

TODAY I SPENT _____ HOUR(S) OFF-SCREEN.

WHAT I ENJOYED MOST FROM MY OFF-SCREEN TIME:

_____

_____

_____

_____

CHALLENGES:

_____

_____

_____

MY OVERALL MOOD TODAY:

- ☐ CHEERFUL
- ☐ CALM
- ☐ LIGHTHEARTED
- ☐ GLOOMY
- ☐ STRESSED
- ☐ ANGRY

- ☐ ANXIOUS
- ☐ TIRED
- ☐ MOTIVATED
- ☐ LAZY
- ☐ REFLECTIVE
- ☐ ROMANTIC

- ☐ HOPEFUL
- ☐ TENSE
- ☐ BORED
- ☐ CONFIDENT
- ☐ GRATEFUL
- ☐ OTHER: _____

FINAL THOUGHTS:

_____

_____

_____

_____

MORNING

GOAL: TODAY, I WILL SPEND _____ HOUR(S) OFF-SCREEN

DAILY OFF-SCREEN PLANNER

EXPLORE	MEET
TIME:	TIME:
MOVE	CREATE
TIME:	TIME:
LEARN	REFLECT
TIME:	TIME:
HELP	PLAY
TIME:	TIME:
PREP	OTHER
TIME:	TIME:

EVENING

TODAY I SPENT _____ HOUR(S) OFF-SCREEN.

WHAT I ENJOYED MOST FROM MY OFF-SCREEN TIME:

_____

_____

_____

_____

CHALLENGES:

_____

_____

_____

_____

MY OVERALL MOOD TODAY:

☐ CHEERFUL   ☐ ANXIOUS   ☐ HOPEFUL

☐ CALM   ☐ TIRED   ☐ TENSE

☐ LIGHTHEARTED   ☐ MOTIVATED   ☐ BORED

☐ GLOOMY   ☐ LAZY   ☐ CONFIDENT

☐ STRESSED   ☐ REFLECTIVE   ☐ GRATEFUL

☐ ANGRY   ☐ ROMANTIC   ☐ OTHER: _____

FINAL THOUGHTS:

_____

_____

_____

_____

MORNING

GOAL: TODAY, I WILL SPEND ____ HOUR(S) OFF-SCREE

DAILY OFF-SCREEN PLANNER

EXPLORE	MEET
TIME:	TIME:
MOVE	CREATE
TIME:	TIME:
LEARN	REFLECT
TIME:	TIME:
HELP	PLAY
TIME:	TIME:
PREP	OTHER
TIME:	TIME:

EVENING

TODAY I SPENT _____ HOUR(S) OFF-SCREEN.

WHAT I ENJOYED MOST FROM MY OFF-SCREEN TIME:

_____

_____

_____

_____

CHALLENGES:

_____

_____

_____

_____

MY OVERALL MOOD TODAY:

☐ CHEERFUL   ☐ ANXIOUS   ☐ HOPEFUL
☐ CALM   ☐ TIRED   ☐ TENSE
☐ LIGHTHEARTED   ☐ MOTIVATED   ☐ BORED
☐ GLOOMY   ☐ LAZY   ☐ CONFIDENT
☐ STRESSED   ☐ REFLECTIVE   ☐ GRATEFUL
☐ ANGRY   ☐ ROMANTIC   ☐ OTHER: _____

FINAL THOUGHTS:

_____

_____

_____

MORNING

GOAL: TODAY, I WILL SPEND _____ HOUR(S) OFF-SCREEN

DAILY OFF-SCREEN PLANNER

EXPLORE	MEET
TIME:	TIME:
MOVE	CREATE
TIME:	TIME:
LEARN	REFLECT
TIME:	TIME:
HELP	PLAY
TIME:	TIME:
PREP	OTHER
TIME:	TIME:

EVENING

TODAY I SPENT _____ HOUR(S) OFF-SCREEN.

WHAT I ENJOYED MOST FROM MY OFF-SCREEN TIME:
_____
_____
_____
_____

CHALLENGES:
_____
_____
_____
_____

MY OVERALL MOOD TODAY:

☐ CHEERFUL   ☐ ANXIOUS   ☐ HOPEFUL

☐ CALM   ☐ TIRED   ☐ TENSE

☐ LIGHTHEARTED   ☐ MOTIVATED   ☐ BORED

☐ GLOOMY   ☐ LAZY   ☐ CONFIDENT

☐ STRESSED   ☐ REFLECTIVE   ☐ GRATEFUL

☐ ANGRY   ☐ ROMANTIC   ☐ OTHER: _____

FINAL THOUGHTS:
_____
_____
_____
_____

MORNING

GOAL: TODAY, I WILL SPEND _____ HOUR(S) OFF-SCREEN

DAILY OFF-SCREEN PLANNER

EXPLORE	MEET
TIME:	TIME:
MOVE	CREATE
TIME:	TIME:
LEARN	REFLECT
TIME:	TIME:
HELP	PLAY
TIME:	TIME:
PREP	OTHER
TIME:	TIME:

EVENING

TODAY I SPENT _____ HOUR(S) OFF-SCREEN.

WHAT I ENJOYED MOST FROM MY OFF-SCREEN TIME:

_____
_____
_____
_____
_____

CHALLENGES:

_____
_____
_____
_____

MY OVERALL MOOD TODAY:

☐ CHEERFUL   ☐ ANXIOUS   ☐ HOPEFUL
☐ CALM   ☐ TIRED   ☐ TENSE
☐ LIGHTHEARTED   ☐ MOTIVATED   ☐ BORED
☐ GLOOMY   ☐ LAZY   ☐ CONFIDENT
☐ STRESSED   ☐ REFLECTIVE   ☐ GRATEFUL
☐ ANGRY   ☐ ROMANTIC   ☐ OTHER: _____

FINAL THOUGHTS:

_____
_____
_____
_____

MORNING

GOAL: TODAY, I WILL SPEND _____ HOUR(S) OFF-SCREEN

DAILY OFF-SCREEN PLANNER

EXPLORE	MEET
TIME:	TIME:
MOVE	CREATE
TIME:	TIME:
LEARN	REFLECT
TIME:	TIME:
HELP	PLAY
TIME:	TIME:
PREP	OTHER
TIME:	TIME:

EVENING

TODAY I SPENT _____ HOUR(S) OFF-SCREEN.

WHAT I ENJOYED MOST FROM MY OFF-SCREEN TIME:
_____
_____
_____
_____
_____

CHALLENGES:
_____
_____
_____
_____

MY OVERALL MOOD TODAY:

☐ CHEERFUL   ☐ ANXIOUS   ☐ HOPEFUL
☐ CALM   ☐ TIRED   ☐ TENSE
☐ LIGHTHEARTED   ☐ MOTIVATED   ☐ BORED
☐ GLOOMY   ☐ LAZY   ☐ CONFIDENT
☐ STRESSED   ☐ REFLECTIVE   ☐ GRATEFUL
☐ ANGRY   ☐ ROMANTIC   ☐ OTHER: _____

FINAL THOUGHTS:
_____
_____
_____
_____

MORNING

GOAL: TODAY, I WILL SPEND _____ HOUR(S) OFF-SCREEN

DAILY OFF-SCREEN PLANNER

EXPLORE	MEET
TIME:	TIME:
MOVE	CREATE
TIME:	TIME:
LEARN	REFLECT
TIME:	TIME:
HELP	PLAY
TIME:	TIME:
PREP	OTHER
TIME:	TIME:

EVENING

TODAY I SPENT _____ HOUR(S) OFF-SCREEN.

WHAT I ENJOYED MOST FROM MY OFF-SCREEN TIME:
_____
_____
_____
_____

CHALLENGES:
_____
_____
_____
_____

MY OVERALL MOOD TODAY:

- ☐ CHEERFUL
- ☐ CALM
- ☐ LIGHTHEARTED
- ☐ GLOOMY
- ☐ STRESSED
- ☐ ANGRY

- ☐ ANXIOUS
- ☐ TIRED
- ☐ MOTIVATED
- ☐ LAZY
- ☐ REFLECTIVE
- ☐ ROMANTIC

- ☐ HOPEFUL
- ☐ TENSE
- ☐ BORED
- ☐ CONFIDENT
- ☐ GRATEFUL
- ☐ OTHER: _____

FINAL THOUGHTS:
_____
_____
_____
_____

MORNING

GOAL: TODAY, I WILL SPEND _____ HOUR(S) OFF-SCREEN

DAILY OFF-SCREEN PLANNER

EXPLORE TIME:	MEET TIME:
MOVE TIME:	CREATE TIME:
LEARN TIME:	REFLECT TIME:
HELP TIME:	PLAY TIME:
PREP TIME:	OTHER TIME:

EVENING

TODAY I SPENT ＿＿ HOUR(S) OFF-SCREEN.

WHAT I ENJOYED MOST FROM MY OFF-SCREEN TIME:

_____
_____
_____
_____

CHALLENGES:

_____
_____
_____
_____

MY OVERALL MOOD TODAY:

☐ CHEERFUL   ☐ ANXIOUS   ☐ HOPEFUL
☐ CALM   ☐ TIRED   ☐ TENSE
☐ LIGHTHEARTED   ☐ MOTIVATED   ☐ BORED
☐ GLOOMY   ☐ LAZY   ☐ CONFIDENT
☐ STRESSED   ☐ REFLECTIVE   ☐ GRATEFUL
☐ ANGRY   ☐ ROMANTIC   ☐ OTHER: ＿＿＿＿

FINAL THOUGHTS:

_____
_____
_____

MORNING

GOAL: TODAY, I WILL SPEND _____ HOUR(S) OFF-SCREEN

DAILY OFF-SCREEN PLANNER

EXPLORE	MEET
TIME:	TIME:
MOVE	CREATE
TIME:	TIME:
LEARN	REFLECT
TIME:	TIME:
HELP	PLAY
TIME:	TIME:
PREP	OTHER
TIME:	TIME:

EVENING

TODAY I SPENT _____ HOUR(S) OFF-SCREEN.

WHAT I ENJOYED MOST FROM MY OFF-SCREEN TIME:

_____
_____
_____
_____

CHALLENGES:

_____
_____
_____
_____

MY OVERALL MOOD TODAY:

☐ CHEERFUL   ☐ ANXIOUS   ☐ HOPEFUL
☐ CALM   ☐ TIRED   ☐ TENSE
☐ LIGHTHEARTED ☐ MOTIVATED   ☐ BORED
☐ GLOOMY   ☐ LAZY   ☐ CONFIDENT
☐ STRESSED   ☐ REFLECTIVE   ☐ GRATEFUL
☐ ANGRY   ☐ ROMANTIC   ☐ OTHER: _____

FINAL THOUGHTS:

_____
_____
_____

MORNING

DATE _/_/_

GOAL: TODAY, I WILL SPEND _____ HOUR(S) OFF-SCREEN

DAILY OFF-SCREEN PLANNER

EXPLORE	MEET
TIME:	TIME:
MOVE	CREATE
TIME:	TIME:
LEARN	REFLECT
TIME:	TIME:
HELP	PLAY
TIME:	TIME:
PREP	OTHER
TIME:	TIME:

EVENING

TODAY I SPENT _____ HOUR(S) OFF-SCREEN.

WHAT I ENJOYED MOST FROM MY OFF-SCREEN TIME:
_____
_____
_____
_____

CHALLENGES:
_____
_____
_____
_____

MY OVERALL MOOD TODAY:

☐ CHEERFUL   ☐ ANXIOUS   ☐ HOPEFUL
☐ CALM   ☐ TIRED   ☐ TENSE
☐ LIGHTHEARTED   ☐ MOTIVATED   ☐ BORED
☐ GLOOMY   ☐ LAZY   ☐ CONFIDENT
☐ STRESSED   ☐ REFLECTIVE   ☐ GRATEFUL
☐ ANGRY   ☐ ROMANTIC   ☐ OTHER: _____

FINAL THOUGHTS:
_____
_____
_____

MORNING

GOAL: TODAY, I WILL SPEND _____ HOUR(S) OFF-SCREEN

DAILY OFF-SCREEN PLANNER

EXPLORE	MEET
TIME:	TIME:
MOVE	CREATE
TIME:	TIME:
LEARN	REFLECT
TIME:	TIME:
HELP	PLAY
TIME:	TIME:
PREP	OTHER
TIME:	TIME:

EVENING

TODAY I SPENT _____ HOUR(S) OFF-SCREEN.

WHAT I ENJOYED MOST FROM MY OFF-SCREEN TIME:

_____

_____

_____

_____

CHALLENGES:

_____

_____

_____

_____

MY OVERALL MOOD TODAY:

☐ CHEERFUL   ☐ ANXIOUS   ☐ HOPEFUL

☐ CALM   ☐ TIRED   ☐ TENSE

☐ LIGHTHEARTED   ☐ MOTIVATED   ☐ BORED

☐ GLOOMY   ☐ LAZY   ☐ CONFIDENT

☐ STRESSED   ☐ REFLECTIVE   ☐ GRATEFUL

☐ ANGRY   ☐ ROMANTIC   ☐ OTHER: _____

FINAL THOUGHTS:

_____

_____

_____

MORNING

GOAL: TODAY, I WILL SPEND _____ HOUR(S) OFF-SCREEN

DAILY OFF-SCREEN PLANNER

EXPLORE	MEET
TIME:	TIME:
MOVE	CREATE
TIME:	TIME:
LEARN	REFLECT
TIME:	TIME:
HELP	PLAY
TIME:	TIME:
PREP	OTHER
TIME:	TIME:

EVENING

TODAY I SPENT _____ HOUR(S) OFF-SCREEN.

WHAT I ENJOYED MOST FROM MY OFF-SCREEN TIME:
_____
_____
_____
_____

CHALLENGES:
_____
_____
_____
_____

MY OVERALL MOOD TODAY:

☐ CHEERFUL   ☐ ANXIOUS   ☐ HOPEFUL

☐ CALM   ☐ TIRED   ☐ TENSE

☐ LIGHTHEARTED   ☐ MOTIVATED   ☐ BORED

☐ GLOOMY   ☐ LAZY   ☐ CONFIDENT

☐ STRESSED   ☐ REFLECTIVE   ☐ GRATEFUL

☐ ANGRY   ☐ ROMANTIC   ☐ OTHER: _____

FINAL THOUGHTS:
_____
_____
_____
_____

MORNING

GOAL: TODAY, I WILL SPEND _____ HOUR(S) OFF-SCREEN

DAILY OFF-SCREEN PLANNER

EXPLORE	MEET
TIME:	TIME:
MOVE	CREATE
TIME:	TIME:
LEARN	REFLECT
TIME:	TIME:
HELP	PLAY
TIME:	TIME:
PREP	OTHER
TIME:	TIME:

EVENING

TODAY I SPENT _____ HOUR(S) OFF-SCREEN.

WHAT I ENJOYED MOST FROM MY OFF-SCREEN TIME:
_____
_____
_____
_____

CHALLENGES:
_____
_____
_____

MY OVERALL MOOD TODAY:

☐ CHEERFUL   ☐ ANXIOUS   ☐ HOPEFUL
☐ CALM   ☐ TIRED   ☐ TENSE
☐ LIGHTHEARTED   ☐ MOTIVATED   ☐ BORED
☐ GLOOMY   ☐ LAZY   ☐ CONFIDENT
☐ STRESSED   ☐ REFLECTIVE   ☐ GRATEFUL
☐ ANGRY   ☐ ROMANTIC   ☐ OTHER: _____

FINAL THOUGHTS:
_____
_____
_____
_____
_____

MORNING

GOAL: TODAY, I WILL SPEND _____ HOUR(S) OFF-SCREEN

DAILY OFF-SCREEN PLANNER

EXPLORE	MEET
TIME:	TIME:
MOVE	CREATE
TIME:	TIME:
LEARN	REFLECT
TIME:	TIME:
HELP	PLAY
TIME:	TIME:
PREP	OTHER
TIME:	TIME:

EVENING

TODAY I SPENT _____ HOUR(S) OFF-SCREEN.

WHAT I ENJOYED MOST FROM MY OFF-SCREEN TIME:

_____

_____

_____

_____

CHALLENGES:

_____

_____

_____

_____

MY OVERALL MOOD TODAY:

☐ CHEERFUL   ☐ ANXIOUS   ☐ HOPEFUL
☐ CALM   ☐ TIRED   ☐ TENSE
☐ LIGHTHEARTED ☐ MOTIVATED   ☐ BORED
☐ GLOOMY   ☐ LAZY   ☐ CONFIDENT
☐ STRESSED   ☐ REFLECTIVE   ☐ GRATEFUL
☐ ANGRY   ☐ ROMANTIC   ☐ OTHER: _____

FINAL THOUGHTS:

_____

_____

_____

_____

MORNING

GOAL: TODAY, I WILL SPEND _____ HOUR(S) OFF-SCREEN

DAILY OFF-SCREEN PLANNER

EXPLORE	MEET
TIME:	TIME:
MOVE	CREATE
TIME:	TIME:
LEARN	REFLECT
TIME:	TIME:
HELP	PLAY
TIME:	TIME:
PREP	OTHER
TIME:	TIME:

EVENING

TODAY I SPENT _____ HOUR(S) OFF-SCREEN.

WHAT I ENJOYED MOST FROM MY OFF-SCREEN TIME:

_____

_____

_____

CHALLENGES:

_____

_____

_____

MY OVERALL MOOD TODAY:

- [ ] CHEERFUL
- [ ] CALM
- [ ] LIGHTHEARTED
- [ ] GLOOMY
- [ ] STRESSED
- [ ] ANGRY

- [ ] ANXIOUS
- [ ] TIRED
- [ ] MOTIVATED
- [ ] LAZY
- [ ] REFLECTIVE
- [ ] ROMANTIC

- [ ] HOPEFUL
- [ ] TENSE
- [ ] BORED
- [ ] CONFIDENT
- [ ] GRATEFUL
- [ ] OTHER: _____

FINAL THOUGHTS:

_____

_____

_____

_____

MORNING

GOAL: TODAY, I WILL SPEND _____ HOUR(S) OFF-SCREEN

DAILY OFF-SCREEN PLANNER

EXPLORE TIME:	MEET TIME:
MOVE TIME:	CREATE TIME:
LEARN TIME:	REFLECT TIME:
HELP TIME:	PLAY TIME:
PREP TIME:	OTHER TIME:

EVENING

TODAY I SPENT _____ HOUR(S) OFF-SCREEN.

WHAT I ENJOYED MOST FROM MY OFF-SCREEN TIME:
_____
_____
_____
_____

CHALLENGES:
_____
_____
_____

MY OVERALL MOOD TODAY:

☐ CHEERFUL   ☐ ANXIOUS   ☐ HOPEFUL
☐ CALM   ☐ TIRED   ☐ TENSE
☐ LIGHTHEARTED   ☐ MOTIVATED   ☐ BORED
☐ GLOOMY   ☐ LAZY   ☐ CONFIDENT
☐ STRESSED   ☐ REFLECTIVE   ☐ GRATEFUL
☐ ANGRY   ☐ ROMANTIC   ☐ OTHER: _____

FINAL THOUGHTS:
_____
_____
_____
_____
_____

MORNING

GOAL: TODAY, I WILL SPEND _____ HOUR(S) OFF-SCREEN

DAILY OFF-SCREEN PLANNER

EXPLORE	MEET
TIME:	TIME:
MOVE	CREATE
TIME:	TIME:
LEARN	REFLECT
TIME:	TIME:
HELP	PLAY
TIME:	TIME:
PREP	OTHER
TIME:	TIME:

EVENING

TODAY I SPENT _____ HOUR(S) OFF-SCREEN.

WHAT I ENJOYED MOST FROM MY OFF-SCREEN TIME:
_____
_____
_____
_____

CHALLENGES:
_____
_____
_____
_____

MY OVERALL MOOD TODAY:

☐ CHEERFUL   ☐ ANXIOUS   ☐ HOPEFUL
☐ CALM   ☐ TIRED   ☐ TENSE
☐ LIGHTHEARTED   ☐ MOTIVATED   ☐ BORED
☐ GLOOMY   ☐ LAZY   ☐ CONFIDENT
☐ STRESSED   ☐ REFLECTIVE   ☐ GRATEFUL
☐ ANGRY   ☐ ROMANTIC   ☐ OTHER: _____

FINAL THOUGHTS:
_____
_____
_____
_____

MORNING

GOAL: TODAY, I WILL SPEND _____ HOUR(S) OFF-SCREEN

DAILY OFF-SCREEN PLANNER

EXPLORE	MEET
TIME:	TIME:
MOVE	CREATE
TIME:	TIME:
LEARN	REFLECT
TIME:	TIME:
HELP	PLAY
TIME:	TIME:
PREP	OTHER
TIME:	TIME:

EVENING

TODAY I SPENT _____ HOUR(S) OFF-SCREEN.

WHAT I ENJOYED MOST FROM MY OFF-SCREEN TIME:
_____
_____
_____
_____

CHALLENGES:
_____
_____
_____

MY OVERALL MOOD TODAY:

☐ CHEERFUL   ☐ ANXIOUS   ☐ HOPEFUL

☐ CALM   ☐ TIRED   ☐ TENSE

☐ LIGHTHEARTED   ☐ MOTIVATED   ☐ BORED

☐ GLOOMY   ☐ LAZY   ☐ CONFIDENT

☐ STRESSED   ☐ REFLECTIVE   ☐ GRATEFUL

☐ ANGRY   ☐ ROMANTIC   ☐ OTHER: _____

FINAL THOUGHTS:
_____
_____
_____
_____

MORNING

GOAL: TODAY, I WILL SPEND _____ HOUR(S) OFF-SCREEN

DAILY OFF-SCREEN PLANNER

EXPLORE	MEET
TIME:	TIME:
MOVE	CREATE
TIME:	TIME:
LEARN	REFLECT
TIME:	TIME:
HELP	PLAY
TIME:	TIME:
PREP	OTHER
TIME:	TIME:

EVENING

TODAY I SPENT _____ HOUR(S) OFF-SCREEN.

WHAT I ENJOYED MOST FROM MY OFF-SCREEN TIME:

CHALLENGES:

MY OVERALL MOOD TODAY:

- ☐ CHEERFUL
- ☐ CALM
- ☐ LIGHTHEARTED
- ☐ GLOOMY
- ☐ STRESSED
- ☐ ANGRY

- ☐ ANXIOUS
- ☐ TIRED
- ☐ MOTIVATED
- ☐ LAZY
- ☐ REFLECTIVE
- ☐ ROMANTIC

- ☐ HOPEFUL
- ☐ TENSE
- ☐ BORED
- ☐ CONFIDENT
- ☐ GRATEFUL
- ☐ OTHER: _____

FINAL THOUGHTS:

MORNING

GOAL: TODAY, I WILL SPEND _____ HOUR(S) OFF-SCREEN

DAILY OFF-SCREEN PLANNER

EXPLORE	MEET
TIME:	TIME:
MOVE	CREATE
TIME:	TIME:
LEARN	REFLECT
TIME:	TIME:
HELP	PLAY
TIME:	TIME:
PREP	OTHER
TIME:	TIME:

EVENING

TODAY I SPENT _____ HOUR(S) OFF-SCREEN.

WHAT I ENJOYED MOST FROM MY OFF-SCREEN TIME:
_____

_____

_____

_____

CHALLENGES:
_____

_____

_____

_____

MY OVERALL MOOD TODAY:

☐ CHEERFUL   ☐ ANXIOUS   ☐ HOPEFUL
☐ CALM   ☐ TIRED   ☐ TENSE
☐ LIGHTHEARTED   ☐ MOTIVATED   ☐ BORED
☐ GLOOMY   ☐ LAZY   ☐ CONFIDENT
☐ STRESSED   ☐ REFLECTIVE   ☐ GRATEFUL
☐ ANGRY   ☐ ROMANTIC   ☐ OTHER: _____

FINAL THOUGHTS:
_____

_____

_____

_____

MORNING

DATE _/_/_

GOAL: TODAY, I WILL SPEND _____ HOUR(S) OFF-SCREEN

DAILY OFF-SCREEN PLANNER

EXPLORE	MEET
TIME:	TIME:
MOVE	CREATE
TIME:	TIME:
LEARN	REFLECT
TIME:	TIME:
HELP	PLAY
TIME:	TIME:
PREP	OTHER
TIME:	TIME:

EVENING

TODAY I SPENT _____ HOUR(S) OFF-SCREEN.

WHAT I ENJOYED MOST FROM MY OFF-SCREEN TIME:
_____
_____
_____
_____

CHALLENGES:
_____
_____
_____
_____

MY OVERALL MOOD TODAY:

- ☐ CHEERFUL
- ☐ CALM
- ☐ LIGHTHEARTED
- ☐ GLOOMY
- ☐ STRESSED
- ☐ ANGRY

- ☐ ANXIOUS
- ☐ TIRED
- ☐ MOTIVATED
- ☐ LAZY
- ☐ REFLECTIVE
- ☐ ROMANTIC

- ☐ HOPEFUL
- ☐ TENSE
- ☐ BORED
- ☐ CONFIDENT
- ☐ GRATEFUL
- ☐ OTHER: _____

FINAL THOUGHTS:
_____
_____
_____
_____

MORNING

GOAL: TODAY, I WILL SPEND _____ HOUR(S) OFF-SCREEN

DAILY OFF-SCREEN PLANNER

EXPLORE	MEET
TIME:	TIME:
MOVE	CREATE
TIME:	TIME:
LEARN	REFLECT
TIME:	TIME:
HELP	PLAY
TIME:	TIME:
PREP	OTHER
TIME:	TIME:

EVENING

TODAY I SPENT _____ HOUR(S) OFF-SCREEN.

WHAT I ENJOYED MOST FROM MY OFF-SCREEN TIME:
_____
_____
_____
_____
_____

CHALLENGES:
_____
_____
_____
_____

MY OVERALL MOOD TODAY:

☐ CHEERFUL   ☐ ANXIOUS   ☐ HOPEFUL
☐ CALM   ☐ TIRED   ☐ TENSE
☐ LIGHTHEARTED   ☐ MOTIVATED   ☐ BORED
☐ GLOOMY   ☐ LAZY   ☐ CONFIDENT
☐ STRESSED   ☐ REFLECTIVE   ☐ GRATEFUL
☐ ANGRY   ☐ ROMANTIC   ☐ OTHER: _____

FINAL THOUGHTS:
_____
_____
_____
_____

MORNING

GOAL: TODAY, I WILL SPEND _____ HOUR(S) OFF-SCREEN

DAILY OFF-SCREEN PLANNER

EXPLORE	MEET
TIME:	TIME:
MOVE	CREATE
TIME:	TIME:
LEARN	REFLECT
TIME:	TIME:
HELP	PLAY
TIME:	TIME:
PREP	OTHER
TIME:	TIME:

EVENING

TODAY I SPENT _____ HOUR(S) OFF-SCREEN.

WHAT I ENJOYED MOST FROM MY OFF-SCREEN TIME:
_____
_____
_____
_____
_____

CHALLENGES:
_____
_____
_____
_____

MY OVERALL MOOD TODAY:

☐ CHEERFUL   ☐ ANXIOUS   ☐ HOPEFUL
☐ CALM   ☐ TIRED   ☐ TENSE
☐ LIGHTHEARTED   ☐ MOTIVATED   ☐ BORED
☐ GLOOMY   ☐ LAZY   ☐ CONFIDENT
☐ STRESSED   ☐ REFLECTIVE   ☐ GRATEFUL
☐ ANGRY   ☐ ROMANTIC   ☐ OTHER: _____

FINAL THOUGHTS:
_____
_____
_____
_____
_____

MORNING

GOAL: TODAY, I WILL SPEND _____ HOUR(S) OFF-SCREEN

DAILY OFF-SCREEN PLANNER

EXPLORE	MEET
TIME:	TIME:
MOVE	CREATE
TIME:	TIME:
LEARN	REFLECT
TIME:	TIME:
HELP	PLAY
TIME:	TIME:
PREP	OTHER
TIME:	TIME:

EVENING

TODAY I SPENT _____ HOUR(S) OFF-SCREEN.

WHAT I ENJOYED MOST FROM MY OFF-SCREEN TIME:

_____

_____

_____

_____

_____

CHALLENGES:

_____

_____

_____

_____

MY OVERALL MOOD TODAY:

- ☐ CHEERFUL
- ☐ CALM
- ☐ LIGHTHEARTED
- ☐ GLOOMY
- ☐ STRESSED
- ☐ ANGRY

- ☐ ANXIOUS
- ☐ TIRED
- ☐ MOTIVATED
- ☐ LAZY
- ☐ REFLECTIVE
- ☐ ROMANTIC

- ☐ HOPEFUL
- ☐ TENSE
- ☐ BORED
- ☐ CONFIDENT
- ☐ GRATEFUL
- ☐ OTHER: _____

FINAL THOUGHTS:

_____

_____

_____

_____

_____

MORNING

GOAL: TODAY, I WILL SPEND _____ HOUR(S) OFF-SCREEN

DAILY OFF-SCREEN PLANNER

EXPLORE	MEET
TIME:	TIME:
MOVE	CREATE
TIME:	TIME:
LEARN	REFLECT
TIME:	TIME:
HELP	PLAY
TIME:	TIME:
PREP	OTHER
TIME:	TIME:

EVENING

TODAY I SPENT _____ HOUR(S) OFF-SCREEN.

WHAT I ENJOYED MOST FROM MY OFF-SCREEN TIME:

CHALLENGES:

MY OVERALL MOOD TODAY:

- ☐ CHEERFUL
- ☐ CALM
- ☐ LIGHTHEARTED
- ☐ GLOOMY
- ☐ STRESSED
- ☐ ANGRY

- ☐ ANXIOUS
- ☐ TIRED
- ☐ MOTIVATED
- ☐ LAZY
- ☐ REFLECTIVE
- ☐ ROMANTIC

- ☐ HOPEFUL
- ☐ TENSE
- ☐ BORED
- ☐ CONFIDENT
- ☐ GRATEFUL
- ☐ OTHER: _____

FINAL THOUGHTS:

MORNING

GOAL: TODAY, I WILL SPEND _____ HOUR(S) OFF-SCREEN

DAILY OFF-SCREEN PLANNER

EXPLORE	MEET
TIME:	TIME:
MOVE	CREATE
TIME:	TIME:
LEARN	REFLECT
TIME:	TIME:
HELP	PLAY
TIME:	TIME:
PREP	OTHER
TIME:	TIME:

EVENING

TODAY I SPENT _____ HOUR(S) OFF-SCREEN.

WHAT I ENJOYED MOST FROM MY OFF-SCREEN TIME:
_____
_____
_____
_____

CHALLENGES:
_____
_____
_____
_____

MY OVERALL MOOD TODAY:

☐ CHEERFUL   ☐ ANXIOUS   ☐ HOPEFUL
☐ CALM   ☐ TIRED   ☐ TENSE
☐ LIGHTHEARTED   ☐ MOTIVATED   ☐ BORED
☐ GLOOMY   ☐ LAZY   ☐ CONFIDENT
☐ STRESSED   ☐ REFLECTIVE   ☐ GRATEFUL
☐ ANGRY   ☐ ROMANTIC   ☐ OTHER: _____

FINAL THOUGHTS:
_____
_____
_____
_____

MORNING

GOAL: TODAY, I WILL SPEND _____ HOUR(S) OFF-SCREEN

DAILY OFF-SCREEN PLANNER

EXPLORE	MEET
TIME:	TIME:
MOVE	CREATE
TIME:	TIME:
LEARN	REFLECT
TIME:	TIME:
HELP	PLAY
TIME:	TIME:
PREP	OTHER
TIME:	TIME:

EVENING

TODAY I SPENT _____ HOUR(S) OFF-SCREEN.

WHAT I ENJOYED MOST FROM MY OFF-SCREEN TIME:

CHALLENGES:

MY OVERALL MOOD TODAY:

☐ CHEERFUL   ☐ ANXIOUS   ☐ HOPEFUL
☐ CALM   ☐ TIRED   ☐ TENSE
☐ LIGHTHEARTED   ☐ MOTIVATED   ☐ BORED
☐ GLOOMY   ☐ LAZY   ☐ CONFIDENT
☐ STRESSED   ☐ REFLECTIVE   ☐ GRATEFUL
☐ ANGRY   ☐ ROMANTIC   ☐ OTHER: _____

FINAL THOUGHTS:

MORNING

GOAL: TODAY, I WILL SPEND _____ HOUR(S) OFF-SCREEN

DAILY OFF-SCREEN PLANNER

EXPLORE	MEET
TIME:	TIME:
MOVE	CREATE
TIME:	TIME:
LEARN	REFLECT
TIME:	TIME:
HELP	PLAY
TIME:	TIME:
PREP	OTHER
TIME:	TIME:

EVENING

TODAY I SPENT _____ HOUR(S) OFF-SCREEN.

WHAT I ENJOYED MOST FROM MY OFF-SCREEN TIME:
_____
_____
_____
_____
_____

CHALLENGES:
_____
_____
_____
_____

MY OVERALL MOOD TODAY:

- [ ] CHEERFUL
- [ ] CALM
- [ ] LIGHTHEARTED
- [ ] GLOOMY
- [ ] STRESSED
- [ ] ANGRY

- [ ] ANXIOUS
- [ ] TIRED
- [ ] MOTIVATED
- [ ] LAZY
- [ ] REFLECTIVE
- [ ] ROMANTIC

- [ ] HOPEFUL
- [ ] TENSE
- [ ] BORED
- [ ] CONFIDENT
- [ ] GRATEFUL
- [ ] OTHER: _____

FINAL THOUGHTS:
_____
_____
_____
_____

MORNING

GOAL: TODAY, I WILL SPEND _____ HOUR(S) OFF-SCREEN

DAILY OFF-SCREEN PLANNER

EXPLORE	MEET
TIME:	TIME:
MOVE	CREATE
TIME:	TIME:
LEARN	REFLECT
TIME:	TIME:
HELP	PLAY
TIME:	TIME:
PREP	OTHER
TIME:	TIME:

EVENING

TODAY I SPENT _____ HOUR(S) OFF-SCREEN.

WHAT I ENJOYED MOST FROM MY OFF-SCREEN TIME:

CHALLENGES:

MY OVERALL MOOD TODAY:

☐ CHEERFUL   ☐ ANXIOUS   ☐ HOPEFUL
☐ CALM   ☐ TIRED   ☐ TENSE
☐ LIGHTHEARTED   ☐ MOTIVATED   ☐ BORED
☐ GLOOMY   ☐ LAZY   ☐ CONFIDENT
☐ STRESSED   ☐ REFLECTIVE   ☐ GRATEFUL
☐ ANGRY   ☐ ROMANTIC   ☐ OTHER: _____

FINAL THOUGHTS:

INSIGHTS

A Mandala Journal

MANDALA
PUBLISHING

www.mandalaearth.com
Tag us on Instagram! @mandalaearth